Sourdough Cookbook for Beginners

Mouthwatering Recipes for Homemade Artisan Bread, Pastries, and More

© **Copyright 2024 - All rights reserved.**

The content contained within this book may not be reproduced, duplicated, or transmitted without direct written permission from the author or the publisher.

Under no circumstances will any blame or legal responsibility be held against the publisher or author for any damages, reparation, or monetary loss due to the information contained within this book, either directly or indirectly.

Legal Notice:

This book is copyright-protected. It is only for personal use. You cannot amend, distribute, sell, use, quote, or paraphrase any part of the content within this book without the consent of the author or publisher.

Disclaimer Notice:

Please note the information contained within this document is for educational and entertainment purposes only. All effort has been executed to present accurate, up-to-date, reliable, and complete information. No warranties of any kind are declared or implied. Readers acknowledge that the author is not engaging in the rendering of legal, financial, medical, or professional advice. The content within this book has been derived from various sources. Please consult a licensed professional before attempting any techniques outlined in this book.

By reading this document, the reader agrees that under no circumstances is the author responsible for any losses, direct or indirect, that are incurred as a result of the use of the information contained within this document, including, but not limited to, errors, omissions, or inaccuracies.

Table of Contents

Introduction 1

Chapter 1: Exploring the World of Sourdough 3

Chapter 2: Getting Started with Sourdough 10

Chapter 3: Mastering Sourdough Bread 25

Chapter 4: Beyond the Loaf: Sourdough Pastries and More 40

Chapter 5: Exploring Flavor Combinations 57

Chapter 6: Gluten-Free and Health-Conscious Options 71

Chapter 7: Tips for Successful Sourdough Baking 85

Chapter 8: Sourdough for All: Inclusive and Accessible 99

Conclusion 109

References 111

Introduction

You'll learn everything you need to know to master the art of sourdough baking through reading this book. Baking sourdough from scratch is not just about following a recipe. To achieve the desired results, you must understand the science and processes behind sourdough. Sourdough bread is characterized by its golden, crispy crust, perfectly chewy consistency, soft and warm crumb, and tangy aroma.

Most people are not only hesitant to start baking their own bread, but they also fear making sourdough at home. The idea of creating and maintaining a living culture of wild yeast can be terrifying. Questions like "What if I accidentally let it die?", "What if it goes bad?" or "What if I feed it too much?" can hold you back. However, while it requires a degree of understanding and dedication, making sourdough starter and bread is easier than you might think. Sourdough bread is usually pricier when bought at cafes, bakeries, or supermarkets. This misleads people into thinking that making it requires expensive ingredients to bake. Many people don't realize that you don't need fancy ingredients to make the sourdough starter and that you'll find most of them in your pantry.

Sourdough bakeries have been enjoyed for millennia across different cultures. Baking the bread is a revered tradition that bridges the gap between culinary arts and fermentation science. Reading this book, you'll learn about sourdough baking and the joys and benefits of making it from scratch. You'll also learn about the different types of flour starters, how to create and maintain them, and the essential tools and equipment you'll need. You'll find common sourdough recipes, tips for navigating common baking issues, and guidance on making sourdough pastries beyond bread. This book teaches you to make sourdough pancakes, waffles, pizza, flatbread, sweet pastries, and desserts. You'll also learn to make herb, cheese, fruit, or nut-infused sourdough and understand how to adjust recipes to accommodate gluten-free diets.

This book offers tips on planning and managing your time while making dough from scratch, provides step-by-step instructions for properly storing sourdough, and explains how to revive and repurpose sourdough discards. It's designed to help beginners and seasoned bakers navigate the process easily and calmly deal with common baking issues as they arise. Following this book's steps, tips, and advice will ensure an enjoyable and successful sourdough baking experience and leave you with plenty of delicious pastries to share with your loved ones.

Chapter 1: Exploring the World of Sourdough

Sourdough has been perfected and enjoyed for millennia. The first recorded use of sourdough in bread leavening was in ancient Egypt in 3000 BC. This recipe then traveled to the Greek and Roman empires and gradually spread throughout the rest of Europe. It was also an essential source of nutrition for miners during the Klondike Gold Rush in Yukon in 1896. In this chapter, you will explore the world of sourdough and find a brief overview of sourdough baking. You'll discover why this type of bread is a unique and flavorful choice and why many people enjoy making it from scratch.

Overview of Sourdough Baking

Many people shy away from baking sourdough bread at home, thinking that it's a complex endeavor. After preliminary research, you might think baking this type of bread is for those willing to make it a lifestyle and not for those interested in baking the occasional loaf of bread. Many people feel overwhelmed by the idea of constantly watching and potentially forgetting about their dough starters.

However, baking sourdough can be a fun experience, and it definitely doesn't have to be that serious. With only a few ingredients and the right techniques, you will master the art of sourdough baking in no time. Baking is easy, even if you decide to bake your own bread all the time. This bread's recipes are more or less similar. However, no two loaves will ever come out tasting and looking exactly the same. For good results, you must understand the impact of method and timing and add the right personal touch.

1. Sourdough can be easily baked at home. Source: https://unsplash.com/photos/brown-wooden-chopping-board-with-brown-wooden-spoon-YZtWLZslVFw

Sourdough is essentially low-fermented bread. Instead of commercial yeast, you use sourdough starters, which are live fermented cultures, to get the loaf to rise. You can make the starter yourself, get some from a family member or a friend who bakes or buy it from a reputable source. Using a natural leavening agent makes this type of bread a healthier choice than its store-bought counterparts. The long fermentation process makes the bread more easily digestible by breaking gluten down.

Making a sourdough starter is as easy as combining water and flour. The trick is to feed it regularly to ensure maximum rising. There are numerous ways to feed a starter, and you'll find the one that works for you over time. One method is to keep only half of the culture in the jar and feed it with equal parts flour and water before letting it rest in a warm spot. You know that it's ready to use when it doubles in size and bubbles form. Depending on the temperature and the starter itself, this can take 2 to 12 hours. You don't need to discard the remaining half of the starter. You can simply give it to someone interested in bread baking.

Once done, you use the amount you need for your recipe and continue feeding the rest to keep the process going. When baking it, make sure to follow a reliable recipe. Follow all the steps carefully to get the right measurements and ingredients, ensuring it comes out exactly how you want it to. If you're not ready to bake again, keep it in the fridge to slow down its activity. You can leave it there for around a week before feeding it again.

Why Sourdough Is a Unique and Flavorful Choice

Sourdough bread stands out from other loaves in the market. Imagine biting through its crusty top layer to find it warm and fluffy inside. It offers the perfect amount of chew. Not too much that it feels dry, and not too little so you savor its tangy, superior flavor. It's delicious to consume on its own, yet it perfectly complements nearly every type of cheese or topping you can think of. Aside from its incredible texture and taste, sourdough bread offers a vast array of health benefits.

It's packed with nutrients that your body can easily and instantly absorb. Since fermented bread is easily digested, your body will absorb the phosphate, zinc, potassium, iron, and magnesium in the flour. Regular wheat bread doesn't offer the same benefits as it contains phytic acid, which makes it more difficult for your body to absorb minerals. Since sourdough bread is slow-fermenting, the dough becomes acidified and releases an enzyme (phytase) that helps break down phytic acid, reducing it by up to 90%.

Incorporating this bread into your diet and reducing your intake of other types of bread can help with bloating and digestive discomfort issues. The phytic acid found in regular wheat bread affects the ability of stomach enzymes to break down starch and proteins, leading to digestive discomfort. The phytase released during the fermentation doesn't inhibit the enzymes in the stomach as other types of bread do, making it gentler on the stomach and leading to better digestion.

The gluten content in sourdough bread is also significantly lower than in other types of bread. If you struggle with irritable bowel syndrome or have minor gluten intolerance, which you might not be aware of in the first place, you'll feel a lot better after you give up regular bread for slow-fermented bread. This is because the bread fermentation process also leads to the pre-digestion of gluten. Keep in mind, however, that sourdough is not gluten-free and only reduces the amount of this protein, still making it unsuitable for those who struggle with Celiac Disease.

Sourdough bread contains high amounts of fiber, especially if you bake it using rye, wholegrain, or whole-wheat flour. This allows your body to digest it slowly, meaning that it also has a low glycemic index. Low glycemic index, or GI, refers to types of food that lead to a slower and steadier release of glucose into the bloodstream, stabilizing your blood sugar levels and making you feel more energized throughout the day. Sourdough bread, when baked with certain types of flour, is therefore suitable for those struggling with PCOS and Type 2 Diabetes. It's also packed with prebiotics (fibers) and probiotics, which are beneficial bacteria found in the gut that feed on fiber.

The Joy of Baking Your Own Bread from Scratch

It's not a coincidence that thousands of people developed a newfound passion for baking during the COVID lockdown. Most people tried everything they could think of, from yoga to painting, to manage their stress and keep their sanity. However, evidently, baking was among the most popular activities. According to Hershey's, 30% of consumers developed baking skills during the pandemic, and 34% reportedly practiced it as a form of self-care, and it's all for good reason.

2. *Baking your own sourdough at home is not only easy, but also very enjoyable. Source: https://www.pexels.com/photo/crop-little-girl-with-man-making-dough-with-flour-3807314/*

Many people find comfort in baking because it anchors them to tradition. It's a familiar, old-fashioned practice that offers a sense of familiarity and comfort during times of uncertainty. It's also a way to bring friends and family together by baking or sharing the food you made. It helps slow down the pace of the world around you, offering a temporary break and allowing you to connect with yourself or your family.

Baking is also a therapeutic process because it requires a certain level of focus that distracts you from overwhelming thoughts and feelings without being too mentally demanding. It allows you to reflect on different areas of your life without overindulging. The experience of working with your own hands and engaging your senses also offers a calming effect. You work with different textures, inhale several scents, and watch the dough evolve into bread. Sharing your efforts to cook and eat your delicious food with others is also very fulfilling.

Home baking relieves the stress of finding products that suit your needs because it allows for customization. You can choose the type of flour you wish to use and use whatever grains and seeds you have on hand. When you bake your own food, you also control the ingredients, amounts, techniques, and general cleanliness and hygiene standards. You don't have to worry about additives, excess sugar, and preservatives in store-bought bread.

Making your own bread from scratch isn't a walk in the park. You can easily master it with practice and dedication, but not everyone is willing and knows how to do it. This is why baking and experimenting with different recipes, techniques, and ingredients can offer a sense of accomplishment and boost your self-esteem.

Now that you know the benefits of sourdough and understand that it's not a difficult endeavor, you're ready to start making bread. Aside from its impeccable taste and texture, sourdough bread offers numerous advantages. It boosts your mental health due to its calming and relaxing effects and elevates your physical health because of its low gluten, glycemic index, and probiotic content.

Chapter 2: Getting Started with Sourdough

Sourdough is where the art of bread-making and fermentation science come together. Home bakers are slowly becoming more mindful about embracing slow cooking processes. What better place to start than the good old bread? This chapter will teach you about the sourdough starter and equip you with the essential tools, knowledge, and techniques needed to make the best sourdough. This detailed guide will teach you what a sourdough starter is and how to create and maintain it. You will also learn about the different flours you can use, the equipment you will need, and some additional tips you can use as a beginner.

Understanding Sourdough Starter

First, you must be wondering, "What is a sourdough starter?". A sourdough starter is a culture made by blending wild yeast with suitable lactic acid bacteria. It should be treated as a live entity and must be refreshed by continuously feeding it flour and fresh water. If you take care of it, you can bake countless breads from the same culture. A sourdough starter is essential because it ferments new dough while making bread. It is also responsible for flavoring the loaf of sourdough bread and is used to make the bread rise. Although this natural fermentation process will take longer, the bread will be more complex and flavorful.

How to Make a New Sourdough Starter

It takes a few days to create the best sourdough starter. However, if you need things to speed up, you should create the best environment for the bacteria and yeasts to form. Many bakers have experimented and learned through years of experience that keeping high hydration (100% water to flour in baker's percentages) and the mixture warm at around 80°F (26°C) will help get things started more quickly. Moreover, using certain flours can also increase the chances of your starter taking hold quickly. Here is a step-by-step guide on how you can make your new sourdough starter:

Ingredients:

- 3 ½ ounces of rye or whole wheat flour
- 3 ½ fluid ounces of water

3. Creating the sourdough starter is the first of many steps of baking the perfect sourdough. Source: Jeuwre, CC BY-SA 4.0 <https://creativecommons.org/licenses/by-sa/4.0>, via Wikimedia Commons: https://commons.wikimedia.org/wiki/File:Sourdough_starter_001.jpg

Instructions:

Day 1:

1. Put your clean container on your scale and note how much it weighs.
2. Tare the scale to "0".
3. Add the whole wheat or rye flour to the container.
4. Add the water to the container.
5. Stir properly to ensure that no dry spots are left behind.
6. Cover the container with a loose lid or a paper towel and a rubber band to allow gasses to escape.

7. Set the container in a warm place (70°F - 80°F/21°C to 26°C) for 24 hours.

Day 2:
1. You may or may not notice some bubble formation in the mixture.
2. Remove 3 ½ ounces of the material, leaving you with 3 ½ ounces of starter in the container (discarding process).
3. Add 3 ½ fluid ounces of water to the container.
4. Stir the starter thoroughly to break it up.
5. Add 3 ounces of your rye/wheat flour again (feeding process).
6. Stir so that no dry spots are left behind.
7. Cover the container with a loose lid or a kitchen towel and rubber band again.
8. Set the container in a warm place for 24 hours.

Day 3:
1. Discard 7 ounces from the container, leaving you with 3 ½ ounces.
2. Add 3 ½ fluid ounces of water and stir the starter thoroughly.
3. Add 3 ½ ounces of flour and stir so no dry spots are left in the container.
4. Cover the container with a loose lid and keep it in a warm place for 12 hours.
5. Repeat the process after 12 hours.

6. Any activity that you may have noticed in the earlier days may die down and increase slowly.

Day 4-6:
1. Repeat the feeding process after every 12 hours.
2. The activity in the container may increase gradually.
3. Feel free to blend 1.7 ounces of rye flour with 1.7 ounces of wheat flour.

Day 7:
1. Notice the increased activity in your container.
2. Place a rubber band around the container at the top after you feed the starter.
3. Monitor its growth every 4 to 8 hours after feeding it.
4. The starter will rise depending on the type of flour and the environment.
5. The starter will grow double or triple its height.
6. Upon reaching its peak, the starter will fall back down and leave streaks on the side of the container.
7. Once you notice the above behavior, your starter is ready to bake.
8. If you do not notice any growth, repeat the 12-hour feeding process.

How to Maintain a Sourdough Starter

Once you have finally created your sourdough starter, feed it with fresh water and your preferred flour. This is essential if you plan to use it continuously for your baking endeavors. The best part about maintaining your sourdough starter is that as it gets older, it gets better. However, it is crucial to feed it regularly.

You must take notice of when you think that your starter is hungry. You must pay attention to the activity in the container, especially after the feeding and discarding process, once it reaches its peak. You will have to do it every four to six hours. However, if you have a mature starter, you can't wait to feed it after eight or more hours. It is understandable if you find the discarding process a bit excessive. Please note that you do not have to feed your starter a cup of flour every time you feed it. You can reduce the quantity, especially once your starter is mature and doing well. You can feed it as little as an ounce of flour and water if needed. You can also preserve your starter for short-term or long-term storage.

Short-Term: Store the Sourdough Starter in the Fridge

The starter becomes stronger as it matures, making it easier for you to store it in the fridge for long intervals without feeding it. However, to let this happen, you must slow the fermentation activity, or your natural yeast will die. You can keep your starter at room temperature for an hour or more and then close the container tightly before placing it in the fridge. You can keep the starter in the fridge for over a week before removing it and feeding or discarding it. These feedings will help you activate the starter to ensure it can give your bread a good rise.

Long-Term Storage: Dry the Sourdough Starter

If you want to take a break from feeding your starter so often, or if you want to pass it on to someone else, then you can try drying it. To do this, wait for it to reach its peak, and instead of discarding it, spread it in a thin and equal layer over parchment paper. Let it dry completely, which may take a few days. Then, cut it into smaller pieces and keep them in an airlocked container.

To rehydrate it for your use, you should weigh the starter and crush it into smaller pieces. Then, use the same weight of water to rehydrate it and feed it with an equal weight of flour. You must let it rise and fall. You must continue feeding it until you notice activity again. It may take you up to three feedings before you notice any bubbles. Pay special attention to the sensory clues it gives you rather than sticking to a certain time.

What Is the Best Flour to Start a Starter With?

You can try to make your sourdough with different types of flour and find out which one works best for you. However, seasoned bakers have found that although all flours, from spelt to whole grain wheat, can make a good sourdough starter, whole grain rye flour, and white flour help to speed up the creation of the starter. It works best when the added nutritional value in rye flour is coupled with a highly hydrated and warm mixture. Here are some common flours used for starters:

All-Purpose Flour

All-purpose flour is made with a mixture of soft and hard wheat and has a moderate protein content (around 10-12%). It can easily be found in any supermarket and works well for most starters. It may have a milder flavor than whole-grain flour.

4. All-purpose flour is the most used type of flour globally. Source: https://pixabay.com/photos/flour-grain-food-nourishment-loaf-1581967/

Whole Wheat Flour

Whole Wheat Flour is made from the wheat kernel, which has significantly more protein content (around 13-14%) than the other flours and is richer in nutritional value. It is great for hastening the fermentation process because of its nutritional richness. It will give a nuttier and better flavor to your starter and bread.

5. Made of wheat, whole-wheat flour is less popular yet more nutritious than other types of flour. Source: https://pixabay.com/photos/bread-wheat-flour-food-6486963/

Rye Flour

Rye flour is nutritionally richer than wheat flour, which can help speed up fermentation. It also has a lower gluten content. It can be used often to create an active starter. It is known to add a unique and earthy flavor to your starter.

Depending on their texture and flavor, you can experiment with different flours to find the right one for you. You can also mix different flours in the first few days to help the fermentation stay active. To strengthen your starter, you must try to source locally sourced flour that may have more wild yeasts and bacteria in it.

Essential Tools and Equipment

Your sourdough baking can be done with minimal tools and equipment. However, it helps to have the appropriate tools and equipment ready for making your starter or baking the bread. Here are the essentials that you might need:

Equipment for Starter

1. **Kitchen Scale**: A kitchen scale that measures in pounds and ounces is strongly recommended. You can use it to weigh the starter and feedings or discardings.

6. *It's crucial to use a kitchen scale while making your sourdough starter. Source: https://www.pexels.com/photo/kitchen-scale-and-ingredients-on-counter-8175328/*

2. **Clear Containers**: You must keep one or two clear 320 oz containers. Try to get a glass jar, as it will allow you to observe the activity carefully.

3. **A Stirring Utensil**: Your utensil must be made of plastic, wood, rubber, or silicone to ensure that it does not affect the activity of the starter.

4. **An Instant-Read Thermometer**: This is quite helpful to you get the optimal temperature for your starter.

5. **Rubber Bands**: This measures the height of your starter after feeding and enclosing the container with the kitchen towel.

Equipment for Baking

You will learn more about baking the sourdough bread in detail in the coming chapters, but here is a list of equipment you will need for it:

1. **Dutch Oven**: The Dutch oven will create a steamy environment for your bread, which will give it a crispy crust.

7. *The Dutch oven helps bake your dough better and crispier. Source: https://unsplash.com/photos/white-plastic-container-with-lid-ykqc-EWq9iQ*

2. **Sharp Knife**: This will be needed to score the dough to help the bread expand and give it an aesthetic touch.

3. **Cooling Rack**: This will help the air circulate around the bread after you bake it. This will prevent it from having a soggy bottom and will cool down evenly.

4. **Oven Thermometer**: This helps ensure that the temperature inside the oven is optimal for the bread.

5. **Large Bowl**: This is for combining the ingredients and keeping the dough.

6. **Parchment Paper**: This is for easy transfer of dough from the fridge to the oven.

Sourdough Baking Basics for Beginners

Familiarize yourself with sourdough to make your baking journey less daunting. The sourdough starter process takes around three days in total, but it is quite simple to make. You can use this basic sourdough recipe to make your delicious bread.

Simple Sourdough

Ingredients:

- 3 ½ ounces of active sourdough starter
- 11 ½ fluid ounces of water
- 1 lb. of all-purpose flour (or a mix of bread and whole wheat flour)
- 1 ½ tsp of salt

Instructions:

1. Feed your sourdough starter 4 to 12 hours before starting your dough to ensure it is bubbly and active.
2. Mix the sourdough starter with water in a large bowl and stir until it is dissolved.
3. Add flour and mix until a rough dough is formed.
4. Cover the bowl and let it rest for 30 minutes.
5. Add salt to the dough, gently fold it, and stretch it with your hand or dough scraper.
6. Cover the bowl again to allow it to ferment for 4 to 6 hours at room temperature.

7. Stretch and fold the mixture after every 30 minutes for the first two hours to help develop the gluten structure.
8. After bulk fermentation, put the dough on a floured surface.
9. Give it the shape of an oval loaf, depending on your proofing basket.
10. Place the prepared dough in the floured-proofing basket.
11. Cover the dough and let it rise for 2 to 4 hours at room temperature or in the fridge.
12. The dough will feel puffy and pass the poke test (dough will spring back up after being poked).
13. Preheat your oven to 475°F (245°C) with a Dutch oven inside for at least 30 minutes.
14. Turn out your dough carefully onto the parchment paper.
15. Score the top of the bread with a knife.
16. Place the dough in the preheated oven, cover it with a lid, and bake for 20 minutes.
17. Remove the lid and let it bake for another 20 to 25 minutes until the crust is golden and the bread sounds hollow when tapped on the bottom.
18. Transfer it to a cooling rack to let it cool before you slice it.

Essential Tips for Beginners

1. You must understand that sourdough baking takes time and patience. The long fermentation is what will

create its particular flavor and texture. Don't rush through the process.

2. It is completely fine if your initial few loaves do not turn out to be perfect. You must know that baking is an experience, and you will only get better at it with practice. Allow yourself the grace to learn from the process.

3. Make sure your dough has an appropriate hydration level, as this will impact the texture of the bread. Higher hydration will give you a more open crumb, but achieving it may be tricky. You should start with a moderate hydration level of 70%.

4. The temperature plays a vital role during fermentation. Warmer temperatures will help hasten the fermentation process. Make sure to keep a consistent spot in the kitchen for this process.

5. Try to use locally sourced flours to ensure better results, as these flours usually contain wild yeast and bacteria.

6. Take care of the feeding schedule and monitor the activity.

7. To prevent the dough from sticking to your hands, keep your hands damp.

8. Gentle folding and stretching motions will help develop gluten structure in the dough without tearing it.

9. Scoring the dough will help it expand while you bake, and it also helps you control the direction of the rise. You can try different scoring patterns for aesthetics and functionality.

10. Letting the bread cool down before you slice it is important. This will help set the crumbs and prevent the bread from getting gummy.

Remember that sourdough baking is an art mixed with science. It might take you some time to get your way around it, but with practice, you can hone your skills and enjoy the process of creating delicious sourdough bread.

Chapter 3: Mastering Sourdough Bread

Preparing and keeping all the essentials ready is probably the hardest part of making sourdough bread. The starter itself takes around 10 days to be ready. Compared to that, the actual process of making the loaf is a breeze.

This chapter will help you master the art with an easy recipe. You will learn how to handle any problem that might crop up during and after the process. The artisanal recipes that wrap it up will help you become a professional at making sourdough bread.

Classic Sourdough Loaf

Sourdough bread was invented many centuries ago, and the recipe has undergone several transformations. Nevertheless, the classic recipe has been preserved, a process that gives your loaf the right kind of tang and makes it properly chewy.

Ingredients:

- 1 cup active sourdough starter, made in the previous chapter
- 1 1/2 cups water at room temperature
- 4 cups bread flour
- 2 teaspoons salt

Instructions:

1. Mix the active sourdough starter and water in a large bowl until the starter is dissolved.
2. Add the bread flour and salt. Mix until a rough dough forms.
3. Cover the bowl with a damp cloth and rest for 30 minutes. This is called the autolyze process. Knead the dough by hand for about 10 minutes until it becomes smooth and elastic. Kneading helps develop the gluten in the dough. Ideally, it can develop without kneading, but it will take a lot of time.
4. Place it back in the bowl, cover it, and let it rise at room temperature for three to four hours. Stretch and fold the dough every 30 minutes for the first two hours (for further developing the gluten).
5. Turn the dough out onto a lightly floured surface. Shape it into a round or oval loaf.
6. Place the shaped dough into a proofing basket (or a bowl lined with a floured cloth), seam side up. Cover and let it proof for two to three hours at room temperature, or refrigerate overnight for a longer, slower proof. This is a further resting period for the dough as it rises and leavens one last time.

7. Preheat your oven to 475°F (246°C), even if it's a Dutch oven. It heats the entire oven instead of just the air within.

8. When ready to bake, carefully turn the dough onto a piece of parchment paper.

9. Score the top of the loaf with a sharp knife or razor blade. This will control the direction in which the bread expands while baking.

10. Transfer the dough (with the parchment paper) into the preheated oven. Cover with the lid.

11. Bake for 20 minutes with the lid on. Then, remove the lid and bake for a further 25-30 minutes, or until the crust is deeply golden brown and the loaf sounds hollow when tapped on the bottom.

12. Let the bread cool completely on a wire rack before slicing.

Troubleshooting Common Sourdough Bread Issues

If you are an experienced cook, you will know how rare it is to get any recipe right the first time. Don't be disheartened if your bread doesn't turn out right. Go through the steps again (you may have skipped a few) and give it another try, but if you keep getting the same result, here are the most common troubleshooting tips:

Dense or Heavy Loaf

8. *No one wants a dense loaf of sourdough bread; thus one should try to make it heavy. Source: https://www.pexels.com/photo/photo-of-baked-bread-on-black-metal-tray-1571073/*

Does your bread look flat and dense without a uniform distribution of holes? Does it feel heavy when you pick it up? It may be because the dough hasn't risen enough. Depending on your room temperature, give it enough time to proof. The lower the temperature, the longer the time needed.

If your kitchen is too warm (more than 80°F/26°C), proofing won't take longer than two hours, but if it's too cold (40-50°F/4°C-10°C), it can take around 10 hours. The resulting dough should be about doubled in size.

It's also possible your starter might not be strong enough. Make sure it's bubbly and active before using it. You can feed it for a few days before baking. Additionally, too much flour can make the dough too stiff. Stick to the recipe's measurements and adjust the hydration level if necessary.

Deflated Bread

9. *Your dough should come out heavy and bloated, rather than dense and deflated. Source: https://www.pexels.com/photo/fresh-bread-on-wooden-cutting-board-7693957/*

Does your bread look flat like a waffle instead of getting the desired bloated shape? Leaving the dough to proof for too long can cause it to overproof, resulting in a deflated loaf. Pay close attention to the dough rather than just the clock. It may also be a result of scoring too deep. Your knife's touch should be delicate, like a surgeon's.

Flat or Spreading Loaf

10. *Your sourdough bread should not be flat and spreading. Source: https://pixabay.com/photos/bread-breakfast-sourdough-heart-7041958/*

Is your loaf flat and spreading out in the container like a pie? Inadequate kneading or not stretching and folding your dough enough can lead to a weak internal structure. See that you're kneading for around 10 minutes, and make sure the result is smooth, even dough.

Keep the moisture of the dough in check. Too much water can make it too slack to hold its shape. The hydration level should be no more than 70%, at least in the beginning. You can change it according to your requirements after you have mastered the process.

Lack of Oven Spring

Is your bread not rising in the oven? The dough might need more time to develop before baking. Poke it at regular intervals with a cookie scribe or a large needle. If it springs back slowly, it's ready.

Cold dough can result in poor oven spring. If you have proofed the dough in the refrigerator, let it sit at room temperature for a while before baking. Steam helps the loaf expand. A Dutch oven is perfect for this. Alternatively, you can place a pan of water inside to generate a steady steam.

Crust Too Thick or Too Hard

11. A smooth, soft crust beats a thick, hard one. Source: https://pixabay.com/photos/bread-baked-loaf-bakery-4183225/

Ignore this if you prefer crunchy bread. Ideally, a sourdough loaf's crust is thin and soft. If it's too thick and hard, you're probably baking for too long or at too high a temperature. The presence of steam generates a more crispy, thin crust. You may also have used excess flour in the mix, which could have generated a thicker layer.

Pale Crust

12. A pale loaf lacks the tastiness, freshness, and color of a well-baked loaf. Source: https://pixabay.com/photos/bread-sourdough-sourdough-bread-997529/

Does your loaf look pale, as if it has been sitting around for years? You may not have preheated your oven. The bake time matters for the crust to develop a deep color. Extend it slightly if needed.

However, the main problem may lie with the starter. Natural sugars in the dough contribute to browning. Ensure your starter is well-fed and active to maximize these sugars. Don't overproof because that brings down the sugar levels considerably.

Gummy or Wet Interior

The damp and gummy interior is probably because you sliced the bread too soon. It's understandable you'd prefer warm, fresh bread, but if you don't leave it to cool, you will get a moist, gummy crumb (many prefer it that way!). Also, make sure the bread is baked long enough. A good test is to check the internal temperature of the loaf, which should be around 200°F (93°C).

The dough needs more time to rise before baking. Without proper proofing, you will get a sticky interior. Additionally, if the dough is too wet before baking, the extra water will remain within it, causing it to dampen.

General Tips

- Did you know that weighing ingredients is more accurate than measuring by volume? Use a kitchen scale to weigh them in ounces (mentioned in the recipe) instead of adding cups.
- A healthy, active starter is crucial for good sourdough bread. Feed it regularly. It should be bubbly and active before baking.

- Dough behavior can change with the seasons and your kitchen environment. Be prepared to adjust proofing times and methods according to the climate and room temperature.

Advanced Sourdough Techniques for Artisanal Variations

Once you have made your first deliciously tangy sourdough loaf, you may wonder: what's next? The bread is usually eaten whole with butter or made into a breakfast sandwich, but can you make the loaf even better? Is adding to the traditional tang and chew possible to prepare an even more sumptuous variant? It sure is!

Adding Mix-Ins

You can have the bread as is, but adding a few more ingredients into the mix will make it taste even better.

Ingredients:

- Seeds (sunflower, sesame, flax)
- Nuts (walnuts, pecans, almonds)
- Dried fruits (raisins, cranberries, apricots)
- Herbs and spices (rosemary, thyme, garlic)

Instructions:

1. Prepare the sourdough starter.
2. Mix it with water in a bowl.
3. Add bread flour and salt and mix to form a rough dough.

4. After the autolyze process, knead the dough thoroughly.
5. Add the seeds, nuts, dry fruits, herbs, and spices as needed, and knead a few more times.
6. Add some more after stretching and folding, and stretch and fold once again.

Ensure even distribution to avoid clumping. You can add more ingredients depending on your preferences, but start with these tried and tested ones initially.

Using Whole Grains and Specialty Flours

Do you want to vary your sourdough bread's protein and fiber content? You can change the type of flour used. The taste will also differ slightly.

- **Rye Flour**: Contains 8-12% protein and 15-18% fiber. It has a robust, earthy, slightly tangy taste.
- **Spelt Flour**: Contains 12-15% protein and 10-12% fiber. It has a slightly sweet and nutty flavor.
- **Whole Wheat Flour**: Considered the healthiest of the lot, it contains 13-15% protein and 12-15% fiber. It has a hearty, sweet, and nutty flavor.
- **Einkorn Flour**: Contains 14-18% protein and 10-12% fiber. It has a sweet and nutty taste with a rich golden color.

You should only substitute a portion of bread flour with whole grain or specialty flour, not switch entirely. Start with 10-20% and adjust according to taste. Note that whole grains may require more water due to higher fiber content.

Extended Autolyze

Do you want to improve the gluten development in your dough and enhance the bread's flavor even more? You can do that by extending the autolyze process. Let the mixture of flour and water rest for one to three hours more (than the regular 30 minutes) before adding salt and starter.

Cold Fermentation (Retardation)

Have you developed a taste for sourdough bread and want a more nuanced, deeper flavor? Cold fermentation is the way to go. It also improves dough handling and shaping. After shaping, instead of proofing it at room temperature, refrigerate the dough for 12-24 hours. To avoid a flatter bread, let it come to room temperature for an hour before baking.

Laminating Dough

This is an advanced technique used to incorporate air and add layers to the dough, enhancing the texture and structure of the bread. This method is commonly used in making pastries like croissants but can also be adapted for sourdough bread to create a lighter, more open crumb.

After the first two hours of bulk fermentation, stretching, and folding, your dough should be more elastic.

1. Lightly flour your work surface to prevent sticking.
2. Gently turn the dough out onto the floured surface.
3. Using your hands, stretch the dough into a large, thin rectangle. Aim for a thickness of about 1/8 inch. Be gentle to avoid tearing. If it resists or starts to tear, let it rest for 10-15 minutes to relax the gluten, then continue stretching.

4. Fold the dough into thirds like a letter (one side over the middle, then the other side over the first fold).

5. Fold it into thirds again from top to bottom. This process creates multiple layers within the dough.

Place the laminated dough back into the bowl, cover it, and let it rest for around 30 minutes before continuing with the fermentation.

Creating a Tangzhong or Yudane

These are bread-baking techniques that improve the quality of your dough. Yudane is easier to prepare, but Tangzhong results in a softer structure. Both processes extend the loaf's shelf life. You need to start by cooking a portion of flour and water into a thick paste, cooling it, and incorporating it into the dough.

For Tangzhong baking, measure one part flour to five parts water. For Yudane, mix one part flour with one part boiling water and mix until a thick paste forms.

Artistic Scoring

Creating a basic cross-like pattern on your loaf isn't the only way of scoring. Did you know there is a separate fanbase for uniquely designed scores? Here are a few designs you can try: (Show each type of scoring pattern below)

- **Diamond Crosshatch**: It's simply a series of crossing lines like in tic-tac-toe. After baking, the loaf will look like a sea of lava with a few flat rocks thrown in. While scoring, make sure there's about an inch of space between the lines.
- **Leaf**: This easy and appealing design makes your loaf look like a leaf. Imagine that there is a line in the

middle of your dough. Carve lines on either side of the imaginary one.

- **Spiral**: This is slightly difficult and will need a steady hand. Hold your knife in the middle of the dough. Spin the dough as you move the knife away from the middle. After baking, it will look like the Milky Way galaxy if you squint your eyes.

Let your imagination run wild, and come up with your own designs.

Adding Steam

Steam enhances oven spring and crust development. A Dutch oven is already steamy, but if you have a normal oven, you can use a steam pan or spray water into the oven before you start baking. Alternatively, use a cast iron skillet with boiling water or ice cubes.

Experimenting with Hydration Levels

Did you know higher hydration (75-85%) creates an open crumb and an even chewier texture? Once you have learned how to handle a regularly hydrated dough, increase the water in small amounts during each try (say 72%, 74%, 76%, and so on). You may need to stretch and fold more times to build gluten strength.

Flavor Enhancements

To increase the complexity of the bread's flavor, incorporate fermented grains or seeds (soaked and sprouted). Additionally, you can use water infused with herbs, teas, or spices for subtler flavor variations. You will dive deeper into the world of sourdough flavors in Chapter 5.

Using Preferments (Levain Builds)

Levain is the French name for sourdough bread. There's a small addition you need to make to the classic recipe. Prepare a levain by mixing a small amount of starter with water and flour, allowing it to ferment before adding to the main dough. This boosts fermentation and adds more complexity to the flavor.

Artisanal Recipe Example: Walnut and Cranberry Sourdough

13. There is nothing as delicious as a loaf of walnut and cranberry sourdough bread for bread lovers. Source: https://www.pexels.com/photo/delicious-black-cranberry-bread-on-board-7693940/

The sweet taste of cranberries and earthy walnuts complement the tang of sourdough bread really well. The walnuts also provide an extra crunch on top of the crunchy crust.

Ingredients:

- All the ingredients of the classic sourdough loaf, including starter, water, flour, and salt

- 1/2 cup chopped walnuts
- 1/2 cup dried cranberries

Instructions:

1. Follow the classic dough mixing and autolyze process.
2. After kneading the dough, push some of the walnuts and cranberries into it, then knead some more.
3. After stretching and folding, add the remaining ones and stretch and fold a couple more times.
4. Proceed with bulk fermentation, shaping, and cold retardation.
5. Bake in a preheated Dutch oven at 475°F (246°C) for 20 minutes with the lid on, then 25-30 minutes with the lid off.

Chapter 4: Beyond the Loaf: Sourdough Pastries and More

This chapter is all about going beyond the basic loaf. We're stepping into new territories to explore the exciting world of sourdough pastries, pancakes, and pizzas! You can start your day by making sweet sourdough pancakes, having sourdough pizza for dinner, and delectable sourdough dessert for later. This chapter will help you learn how to churn out wonderful creations just from your sourdough starter. Start exploring the endless possibilities of sourdough baking!

Sourdough Pancakes and Waffles

You can make sourdough pancakes and waffles with an easy sourdough discard recipe. You only need one batter to make waffles or pancakes; how incredible is that? These sourdough pancakes and waffles will bring a delicious change to your breakfast with their mild, tangy flavor. You do not have to worry about the flavor of your pancakes being too strong for you or that it might clash with your toppings or maple syrup. This breakfast made from sourdough starter will bring more richness to it. The waffles also make for an incredible base for savory toppings, such as fried chicken.

14. Sourdough pancakes are much more nutritious and just as delicious as ordinary ones. Source: https://www.pexels.com/photo/pancake-with-sliced-strawberry-376464/

You can mix your sourdough pancake batter and cook it right away, or let your batter ferment overnight to enjoy the flavor and sourdough taste in every bite. Fermenting your batter overnight will also help your pancakes turn out light and fluffy, whereas your waffles will be crispy on the outside and chewy in the center. You can serve your pancakes and waffles with melted butter, maple syrup, blueberries, bananas, or even savory delights like sausage and fried chicken. Your whole family will be delighted to have this breakfast. Make sure that you have a sourdough starter before you start making the batter. You must collect and discard your sourdough starter in a separate container throughout the week. Once you have collected enough discard, you are ready to make these discard waffles and pancakes. This recipe yields 12 pancakes and 4 waffles.

Equipment:
- Mixing bowl
- Griddle
- Waffle Iron
- Whisk

Ingredients:
- 7 ounces of sourdough starter discard (stirred down)
- 8 ½ fluid ounces of buttermilk or milk
- 1.7 ounces of white sugar or honey
- 3/4 tsp of vanilla extract
- 1.9 ounces of melted butter
- 8 1/2 ounces of all-purpose flour
- ¾ tsp of fine sea salt
- 3/4 tsp of baking powder
- 3/4 tsp of baking soda
- 2 large eggs

Instructions to ferment the batter overnight:
1. Before going to bed, whisk together the sourdough starter, melted butter, honey, buttermilk, vanilla extract, and flour in a large bowl.
2. Cover the bowl with a lid and keep the batter at room temperature overnight.
3. Next morning, add eggs, baking powder, salt, and baking soda to the batter and stir it.
4. Keep the batter at rest for 20 minutes before cooking.

Instructions to cook the batter right away:

1. Mix the sourdough starter discard, melted butter, honey, buttermilk, vanilla extract, eggs, baking powder, salt, baking soda, and flour in a large bowl.
2. Let it rest for 20 minutes.
3. Preheat the waffle iron or the griddle.

Instructions for pancakes:

1. Preheat your griddle and lightly grease it with oil or butter.
2. Put ¼ cups of batter onto the griddle in a round shape.
3. Let it cook on one side until you see bubbles forming on the top of the surface and the bottom is light brown or golden.
4. Turn the pancake and continue to cook it on the other side as well until it too, is golden or light brown.
5. Prepare a plate and start stacking your pancakes on it.
6. Add your favorite toppings and serve.

Instructions for waffles:

1. Preheat your waffle iron and grease it with butter or cooking oil spray.
2. Put ¾ cup of batter onto the center and gently spread it out before closing the iron.
3. Cook it for 5 to 6 minutes or till you see light steam coming out (or according to the directions given in your waffle iron's manual).
4. Carefully take your waffle out with a fork or a tong once it's fully cooked.

5. Serve hot with your favorite toppings.

15. With the right topping and positive mood, a sourdough waffle can make your day. Source: https://unsplash.com/photos/cooked-pastries-on-white-plate-GJAHkC6UMfo

Beginner-Friendly Tips

- Make sure your starter is active and bubbly before you use it.
- Do not overmix the batter to keep your waffles and pancakes light and fluffy.
- You can keep the batter in the refrigerator for up to two days before you cook your waffles or pancakes.
- You can also store it in the fridge for up to a week or freeze the batter for up to three months. You can put them in a container or a Ziploc.
- You can also freeze your pancakes or waffles for up to three months. You must separate them with wax or parchment paper and place them in a freezer-safe container.

- You can reheat your pancakes or waffles in the toaster oven for 10 minutes or in the microwave for 60 seconds.
- Reheating them in a toaster oven will help give them a crunchy surface.

Sourdough Pizza Crust and Flatbreads

Sourdough can also fulfill your savory desires. The natural fermentation process that comes with the sourdough starter will improve the flavor and enhance the texture of your pizza crust or flatbread. It will be crispy on the outside and chewy on the inside. If you are craving sourdough pizza or flatbreads, you can easily make them at home.

Sourdough Pizza Crust

Sourdough pizza is one of a kind. It has the perfect crispy and chewy crust that is also light on the stomach! This recipe will help you make the pizza of your dreams really easily. Although it will require a lot of patience on your behalf, don't all good things take time? Start preparing it the night before you want to bake it. You must let the dough ferment on the counter while you sleep and then put it in the fridge in the morning. By evening, your pizza dough will be ready to bake for dinner. Once it's ready, you won't be able to keep your hands off of it. This is what your baking schedule will look like:

Baking Schedule

- **9 PM**: Mix the dough and cover the bowl. Let it sit on the kitchen counter at room temperature for 12 hours.

- **9 AM**: Perform a set of folding and stretching on the dough. Then, cover the bowl and place it in the fridge.
- **6 PM**: Remove the dough from the fridge and let it rest for 30 minutes.
- **6:30 PM**: Your pizza dough is ready to be baked.

16. Even though it takes nearly a whole day to make, a sourdough pizza is worth every minute of making. Source: https://www.pexels.com/photo/fresh-sourdough-pizza-on-plate-10836977/

Equipment:

- Kitchen scale
- Mixing bowls
- Parchment paper
- Cast Iron Skillet

Ingredients:

- 3 ½ ounces of sourdough starter discard
- 1 ¾ tsp of fine sea salt
- 3/4 tbsp of olive oil
- 1 ounce of whole wheat flour
- 15 ounces of all-purpose flour
- 12.3 fluid ounces of water
- Toppings of your choice

Instructions:

1. Add all the ingredients into a large bowl and use your hands to mix it thoroughly.
2. Cover the bowl and allow the dough to ferment for 12 hours.
3. Perform a series of stretches and folds on your dough the next morning.
4. Wet your hands with water to prevent the dough from sticking.
5. Fold one side of the dough to the other and repeat this process until the bowl turns a full circle.
6. Cover the bowl and place it in the fridge until dinnertime.
7. Remove the dough from the fridge when prepping for dinner and let it sit on the counter for 30 minutes at room temperature.
8. Put a generous amount of flour on the workspace where you will cut and divide the dough.

9. Divide the dough into four equal parts and shape each part into a round shape.
10. Cover it all with a kitchen towel and let it rest for 30 minutes.
11. Turn on your oven's broiler and heat your skillet to medium-high heat.
12. As your skillet preheats, gently press the mounds of dough into 6 to 8-inch circles on the floured surface.
13. Put your circle of dough on the skillet and place all the toppings on your crust.
14. Cook for 5 to 6 minutes until the bottom of the crust becomes brown and charred.
15. Place the skillet in the broiler to bake the top of the pizza for 2 to 4 minutes.
16. Once it is ready, remove it from the broiler and cut it into slices.
17. Serve hot and enjoy.

Beginner Friendly Tips

- If you do not have an oven-safe cast iron skillet, you can use a non-stick skillet to cook the pizza on the stove-top.
- Make sure to spray some cooking oil on the nonstick skillet to stop the pizza from sticking.
- Place the pizza on a baking sheet before putting it in the broiler.
- You can let the dough ferment for longer if you want a tangier flavor.

- You may experiment with different flours, such as whole wheat or spelt, to add more depth to the crust.
- Generously flour the workspace to prevent it from sticking.
- Make sure your toppings are ready before you shape the pizza crust because it will be on the stovetop for only a few minutes.
- This recipe will yield four 8-inch pizza crusts.
1. Freezes well and can be used for grab-and-go dinners.

Sourdough Flatbread

This sourdough flatbread recipe is quite easy to make, and you can use it as a pizza base as well. This recipe is great for making sandwich wraps, eating as a side with a soup or salad, as breakfast, or even eating it warm on its own. This bread is quite soft and chewy and bursting with flavor. It can be made with either a sourdough starter or a discard. This sourdough flatbread makes for a great afternoon snack for children and a healthy alternative for satiating your midnight savory cravings.

17. The sourdough flatbread is a popular choice among many sourdough lovers. Source: https://unsplash.com/photos/white-and-brown-pizza-on-brown-wooden-table-ITvUTnRTI6Y

Equipment:

- Kitchen scale
- Large bowl
- Rolling pin
- Cast iron skillet

Ingredients:

- 9.1 ounces of all-purpose flour
- 10 ounces of sourdough discard or 226 g of sourdough starter
- 3.7 fluid ounces of whole milk or dairy-free milk
- 3/4 tsp of baking powder
- 1 tsp of salt
- 1 tbsp of olive oil

Instructions:
1. Add flour, sourdough starter (active or discard), milk, baking powder, olive oil, and salt to a large bowl and mix until flour is completely incorporated.
2. Place the dough on the floured work surface.
3. Stretch and fold the dough by grabbing one side of the dough and placing it on top of the other.
4. Press the heel of your hand onto the dough as you fold it in.
5. Keep turning the dough and stretching and folding it for 2 to 3 minutes.
6. If the dough looks dry, spray some water on it, or if it looks wet, you may add some extra flour to it.
7. Do not worry if it looks a little lumpy.
8. If you use an active sourdough starter, leave the dough in a greased bowl and cover it with a kitchen towel.
9. Let it ferment for 18 hours to 24 hours.
10. If you are using sourdough discard, cover the dough with a kitchen towel, and let it rest for 30 minutes or longer to let the gluten rest.
11. Cut the dough into 8 equal parts with a sharp knife.
12. Sprinkle extra flour on the workspace and rolling pin before you start rolling the dough.
13. Roll one ball at a time, and it should be about ⅛ inch.
14. Cast iron should be preheated at medium heat.
15. Grease the pan with olive oil and place flatbreads on the cast iron individually.

16. Cook until the dough starts to bubble up.
17. Add a bit of olive oil on top before turning to the other side.
18. Cook for 1-2 minutes more and repeat the process on other flatbreads.
19. Serve and enjoy.

Beginner-Friendly Tips

- You may use water or dairy-free milk as an alternative to milk.
- You can also make it in your oven by pre-heating it first.
- Store your flatbread in the refrigerator for 5 days.

Sweet Treats: Sourdough Pastries and Desserts

You can use your sourdough starter to make flavorsome sourdough pastries and desserts. This beautiful treat with flaky layers makes up for the perfect breakfast or dessert treat with your evening tea or coffee. Although it may be a little time-consuming, these amazing puff pastries can be used to make anything, including custard or jam-filled Danish pastries, tarts, pies, etc. It will be worth the patience. You can share it with your loved ones, which will make your moments even sweeter.

Equipment:
- Rolling pin
- Stand mixer

- Pastry brush
- Parchment paper
- Baking sheet
- Large mixing bowl
- Bench scraper

Ingredients:

For Dough:

- 14 ounces of all-purpose flour
- 1.7 ounces of sugar
- 6 ½ fluid ounces of whole milk
- 1 large egg
- ¾ tsp of salt
- 1/2 tsp of vanilla

Butter for Laminating:

- 8 ounces of cold unsalted butter
- 1 ½ tsp of all-purpose flour

Egg Wash:

- 1 large egg (lightly beaten)
- 1 tsp cold water

Instructions:

1. Add all the dry ingredients, milk, egg, vanilla, and sourdough starter to the large bowl.

2. Mix all the ingredients in a stand mixer bowl for 5 minutes on a low speed until it becomes smooth, or knead it by hand until it becomes glossy.
3. Grease a large bowl.
4. Turn your dough into a round shape and place it in the greased bowl.
5. Cover it with foil or wrap and keep it at room temperature for four hours.
6. Put the bowl in the refrigerator and let it ferment for 8 hours to 3 days.
7. On the parchment paper, make a rectangle of 6" by 8".
8. Then, place your butter on the parchment paper and dust it with flour.
9. Now, fold the parchment paper around the butter with the folds on the 6" by 8" rectangle to make a butter package.
10. Tap the butter lightly with a rolling pin, and flatten it out a little.
11. Place the butter package in the fridge and allow it to rest for 10 minutes.
12. Take out the pastry dough from your fridge and place it carefully on the workspace. Make sure that your workspace is generously dusted with flour.
13. Now, spread out the dough into a 16" by 8" inch rectangle.
14. Then, position the butter rectangle in the center of the dough.

15. Start folding towards the center of the dough to enclose the butter.
16. Keep all sides closed by pinching the dough in the middle and ensuring the butter does not escape.
17. Shape it into a rectangle by folding all layers on one another and creating four layers of the folded dough.
18. Wrap your dough in a plastic wrap and let it rest in the fridge for 30 minutes.
19. Then, for your second fold, spread out the dough into a rectangle of 16" by 8" inches.
20. Again, make a rectangle of four layers of dough by folding it onto one another.
21. Then, refrigerate it for 2 hours to 12 hours after wrapping it in a plastic bag.
22. This delectable puff pastry dough may be used to make other delicious desserts.

Beginner-Friendly Tips

- Do not let the dough or butter become too warm during the lamination process.
- Work quickly to maintain a consistent temperature.
- Put the butter or dough in the fridge for 10 to 30 minutes to keep it from getting too warm.
- Place a baking sheet below the pan on the rack to make sure the butter doesn't leak through while baking.

This chapter explored the wonderful capability of sourdough to create nutritious, flavorful, and delicious creations from breakfast to dessert. Although these recipes take longer than usual to cook, there's something about slow and mindful cooking that will make it worth your time. These are beginner-friendly recipes and anyone can make them at home. Remember, with patience comes perfection, don't hesitate to experiment and create your recipes. Happy baking.

Chapter 5: Exploring Flavor Combinations

When you master the art of sourdough, loaf, and other pastries, it's time to try out the new world of flavor combinations for sourdough. When creating flavored sourdough, there are no rights and wrongs. It all depends on your taste and how you like your dough. Some like it sweet, some like it savory, others like combining both. It's up to personal preference what you want to add and how you want to add it. However, there are a few rules to be aware of to get the result you want.

Rules for Adding Flavors to Sourdough

You can try to add dry ingredients in a certain way and create the best sourdough bread of all time, and when you try the same recipe but with a wet ingredient, you create a not-so-nice dough. This happens because wet ingredients can affect the overall hydration of the dough. If you add the same amount of water and then add coffee, milk, frozen fruits, or honey, the hydration ratio will not be disturbed, and the dough might not hold. So, consider the overall hydration ratio when mixing flavors and other ingredients. When it comes to dried fruit, nuts, or any dry ingredient, you don't have to consider the hydration ratio as it won't be affected.

If you're adding raw cocoa, powdered coffee, or any type of powder to the recipe, it's best to add it to the water, mix it, and then add the flour. This way the flavor will be distributed evenly in the dough.

If you feel like experimenting with sugar, remember that sugar will feed the yeast and speed up fermenting time.

When combining new flavors or new methods of creating sourdough, watch your dough more carefully, as some ingredients can have different effects on it.

Adding Flavors

The timing at which you add your flavors to the mix affects the taste of the dough and its distribution. Many people recommend adding any flavor halfway through the stretch and fold. If you're doing 6 sets, add it between the third and fourth fold.

When you add your flavors halfway through the folding, you might see that they are not evenly distributed. However, by the last set of folds, you should see they are all spread evenly.

The main purpose of putting the additions at this stage is to ensure that the dough has enough time for the gluten strands to strengthen and prevent any possible tear from the additions.

Sourdough Texture

Anything you add to your sourdough will change its texture. Some ingredients will make it more moist and harder to work with. However, you can avoid this challenge by drying the flavoring before adding it to the dough.

The texture will change whether you're adding cheese, oats, or anything else, but you shouldn't worry. Just because the texture is not the same as you're used to doesn't mean it will not be good. You just have to find the right texture through experimenting and trial and error.

Different Flavor Combination without Additions

If you're not completely confident with additions to your dough, you can still create different flavors. You can create many flavors by experimenting with flour, water, and fermentation. Here's how you can do it.

Flour Mixes

Each flour type can create a different flavor. You can try different flours, like whole wheat, rye, spelt, and ancient grains. Each one of these flours will create a completely different taste and texture. Some of them will be perfect for different pastries, and others will create sourdough bread with a nutty taste or a robust earthiness. Create, experiment, and try all the flour types and combinations until you find the one you like the most.

Hydration Ratio

The water-to-flour ratio is one factor that greatly impacts the taste and texture of your sourdough, especially if you're making bread. Higher hydration means a more open crumb and tangier flavor, while less hydration can make a thick dough. It's all about trial and error. Try out all the ratios you can think of until you find your preferred balance.

Changing the Starters

You can change from traditional wheat to rye or spelt when adding the starter. Each one of these ingredients will add a special flavor to the dough after its fermentation.

Fermentation Differences

Changing the timing of your fermentation process can have a pleasant impact on the taste of the dough. When you leave it in the fridge longer, it can develop more complex flavors than fermenting it outside.

Sweet and Savory Magic Mixes

Now that you have tried different hydration ratios and flour mixes, it's time to try different additions to your dough and unlock the new flavors. There are endless options for additions, such as sweet, savory, and mixing caramelized onions and sundried tomatoes to chocolate, spices, and herbs.

Dried Fruits and Nuts Sourdough

For this recipe, you can use any kind of dried fruit you prefer, whether it's dried apricots, cherries, or dates. It's a great and healthy mix to have for breakfast with a nice spread of your choice.

Ingredients:

- 7 ounces of foamy sourdough starter
- 24 ½ plus 1.7 fluid ounces (reserved) of warm spring water
- 1.9 lb. of unbleached bread flour
- 3 ½ ounces of whole wheat flour

- 3 ½ tsp of fine sea salt
- 4 ½ ounces of dried golden raisins
- 4 ½ ounces of dried fruit
- 4 ½ ounces of nuts

Instructions:

1. Mix warm water with your bubbly starter in a big bowl. Stir it gently with your fingertips.
2. Add flour to the bowl with the water and starter. Use your hands and a dough scraper to mix everything until no flour is left. The dough should look rough.
3. Let the dough rest in the bowl for 30-40 minutes, covered with a towel.

Adding Fruits and Nuts (about 2 hours)

1. Fold in the fruit and nuts gently after about 30 minutes.
2. Cover the bowl again and let it rest for 30 minutes. Repeat this folding process twice (a total of three sets of 30 minutes rest). The dough should become softer and bigger.

Shaping the Dough (about 1 hour)

1. Lightly flour a surface and scrape the dough onto it. Divide the dough into two roughly equal pieces.
2. Gently fold the edges of each dough piece towards the center to form a round ball.
3. Let the dough balls rest for another 30 minutes, covered with a towel.

Final Shaping and Resting (overnight or 3-4 hours):

1. Flour the tops of the dough balls and flip them over.

2. Fold each side of the dough towards the center one by one, then flip it over again.

3. Gently cup your hands around the dough and pull them towards you to create a round shape. Repeat with the other dough ball.

4. Place each dough ball in a separate bowl lined with a floured dishcloth. Cover loosely with plastic wrap and let it rest in the fridge overnight (8-12 hours) or at room temperature for 3-4 hours.

Baking (about 1.5 hours)

1. Preheat your oven to 475°F (246°C) and place a Dutch oven with the lid inside to preheat as well.

2. Carefully remove the hot pot and place one dough ball on a square of parchment paper. Lower it gently into the pot.

3. Make some shallow cuts on top of the dough with a sharp knife.

4. Put the lid back on the pot and bake for 30 minutes. Then, remove the lid and bake for another 30 minutes. Finally, bake with the oven door slightly open for 10 more minutes.

5. Take out the bread and let it cool completely on a wire rack before cutting into it. Repeat the baking process with the other dough ball.

Herb and Cheese Infused Sourdough

Mixing different types of herbs and cheese into your sourdough makes it full of flavor. You can create many types of dough with different combinations of herbs and cheese.

Choose your favorite type of cheese, but make sure it melts easily, like cheddar or gouda. When it comes to the herbs, you can try rosemary, thyme, oregano, cilantro, or any of your preferred herbs. You can also try more than one type of herb to create a bolder taste.

18. The herb and cheese infused sourdough is truly a wonder for those who never tried it. Source: https://unsplash.com/photos/green-and-brown-vegetable-dish-on-white-ceramic-plate-lqvogj4xdKg

If you want to taste the cheese in chunks every few bites, then you should use cheese cubes. However, use shredded cheese to spread the taste evenly throughout the dough.

Ingredients:

- 7 ounces of foamy sourdough starter
- 24 ½ plus 1.7 fluid ounces of warm water
- 1.9 lb. of unbleached bread flour
- 3 ½ ounces of whole wheat flour
- 3 ½ tsp of sea salt
- 4 ½ ounces of cubed or shredded cheese

- 4 ½ ounces of your choice of herbs

Instructions:

1. Combine the warm water with your bubbly starter in a bowl and use your fingertips to stir it gently.
2. Add the flour and use a dough scraper and your hands to combine everything until all the flour is gone. You should be left with a rough dough.
3. Leave the dough in a covered bowl to rest for 30-40 minutes.

Adding Cheese and Herbs

1. After 30 minutes, gently fold in the cheese and herbs.
2. Cover the bowl again and set it aside for 30 minutes. Do this twice more - it should rest for 30 minutes 3 times. The dough should become softer and firmer.
3. Finish the process and set the dough aside for at least a few hours, preferably overnight.

Shaping the Dough (about 1 hour)

1. Turn the dough out on a lightly floured surface and divide it roughly in half.
2. Working with one piece at a time, fold the edges into the center, forming a ball.
3. Place the two dough balls into a bowl, cover it, and leave them for 30 minutes.

Final Shaping and Resting (overnight or 3-4 hours):

1. Sprinkle flour over the dough balls and turn them over.
2. Once again, fold the sides in toward the center, one at a time, and turn it over again.

3. Place your hands around the dough and gently pull it towards you, creating a ball. Do this with both dough balls.

4. Line 2 bowls with floured dishcloths and place a dough ball in each one. Cover the bowl with plastic wrap and refrigerate for 8-12 hours overnight, or leave it at room temperature for 3-4 hours.

Baking (about 1.5 hours)

1. Put a lidded Dutch oven inside your oven and preheat it to 475°F (246°C).

2. Take the Dutch oven out carefully and place a sheet of parchment paper in the bottom. Put one dough ball on it.

3. Using a sharp knife, make several shallow cuts on the top of the dough.

4. Put the lid back on the pot and bake for 30 minutes before taking the lid off and baking it for another 30 minutes. Then, open the oven door slightly and bake it for 10 more minutes.

5. Remove the bread and place it on a wire rack to cool before you slice it. Repeat with the second ball.

Coffee-Infused Sourdough

For all the coffee lovers out there, this recipe is for you. To ensure an evenly distributed coffee flavor in your dough, dissolve your favorite coffee powder in some water and add it to the mix.

19. If you want a healthy, refreshing treat, a coffee-infused sourdough loaf would do. Source: https://unsplash.com/photos/brown-bread-on-brown-wooden-chopping-board-Nso-zio-tYI

Ingredients:

- 7 ounces of foamy sourdough starter
- 17 ½ plus 1.7 fluid ounces (reserved) of warm water
- 1.9 lb. of unbleached bread flour
- 3 ½ ounces whole wheat flour
- 3 ½ tbsp of fine sea salt
- 7 ounces of coffee mixed with water

Instructions:

1. In a big bowl, mix warm water with your bubbly starter. Use your fingertips to stir it gently.
2. Add flour to the bowl with the water and starter. Use your hands and a dough scraper to mix everything until there's no flour left. It should look like a rough dough. Add the water-coffee mix and stir it a little more.

3. Let the dough rest in the bowl for 30-40 minutes, covered with a towel.

Shaping the Dough (about 1 hour):

1. Lightly flour a surface and scrape the dough onto it. Divide the dough into two roughly equal pieces.
2. Gently fold the edges of each dough piece towards the center to form a round ball.
3. Let the dough balls rest for another 30 minutes, covered with a towel.

Final Shaping and Resting (overnight or 3-4 hours):

1. Flour the tops of the dough balls and flip them over.
2. Fold each side of the dough towards the center one by one, then flip it over again.
3. Gently cup your hands around the dough and pull them towards you to create a round shape. Repeat with the other dough ball.
4. Place each dough ball in a separate bowl lined with a floured dishcloth. Cover loosely with plastic wrap and let it rest in the fridge overnight (8-12 hours) or at room temperature for 3-4 hours.

Baking (about 1.5 hours)

1. Preheat your oven to 475°F (246°C) and place a Dutch oven with the lid inside to preheat as well.
2. Carefully remove the hot pot and place one dough ball on a square of parchment paper. Then, gently lower it back into the pot.
3. Make some shallow cuts on top of the dough with a sharp knife.

4. Put the lid back on the pot and bake for 30 minutes. Then, remove the lid and bake for another 30 minutes. Finally, bake with the oven door slightly open for 10 more minutes.
5. Take out the bread and let it cool completely on a wire rack before cutting into it. Repeat the baking process with the other dough ball.

Pumpkin Sourdough

Pumpkins are great for fall but can also be a delicious mix with your sourdough all year. For this recipe, you can either use canned pumpkin puree or pumpkin puree from fresh pumpkin, and both will provide you with the pumpkin flavor in your dough. However, you should remember that the pumpkin puree will increase the hydration in your dough.

Ingredients:

- 7 ounces of foamy sourdough starter
- 17 ½ plus 1.7 fluid ounces (reserved) of warm water
- 1.9 lb. of unbleached bread flour
- 3 ½ ounces of whole wheat flour
- 4 tsp of fine sea salt
- 8.8 ounces of pumpkin puree

Instructions:

1. Mix warm water with your bubbly starter in a big bowl. Stir.

2. Add flour to the bowl and mix it all together with your hands and a dough scraper. There shouldn't be any flour left, and you should be left with a rough dough.

3. Add the Pumpkin Puree with a bit of honey to the mix.

4. Cover the dough with a clean towel and leave it for 30-40 minutes.

Shaping the Dough (about 1 hour)

1. Sprinkle a little flour on a clean surface and put the dough on it. Use a dough cutter or your hands to divide it in half – it doesn't have to be exact. Fold the dough's edge into the middle, forming it into a rough ball.

2. Leave it aside under a towel for 30 minutes.

Final Shaping and Resting (overnight or 3-4 hours):

1. Put some flour on top of each dough ball and turn them over.

2. One at a time, fold each edge into the middle and turn it over again.

3. Cup the dough gently and pull it toward you, forming a round loaf shape. Do the same with the other.

4. Each dough ball should now go in its own ball with a floured towel, covered with plastic, and left to rest at room temperature for 3-4 hours or in the fridge overnight.

Baking (about 1.5 hours)

1. Turn on your oven to 475°F (246°C) and preheat a Dutch oven with a lid.

2. Once heated, take the Dutch oven out carefully. Put a dough ball onto some parchment paper and place it inside the pot.

3. Make a few cuts on top of the dough – only shallow ones – with a sharp knife.

4. Replace the lid and bake the dough for 30 minutes. Take the lid off and bake for 30 more minutes before opening the oven door a little and baking for 10 minutes.

5. Carefully lift the bread form the Dutch oven and set it aside to cool down. Do the same with the remaining dough ball.

Chapter 6: Gluten-Free and Health-Conscious Options

Bread and pastries are usually avoided in healthy eating plans because of their high carbohydrate and gluten content. However, sourdough can be great for your health.

Fermentation occurs when bacteria and enzymes convert carbohydrates into organic acids. These bacteria are some of the good ones that act as a defense against harmful bacteria. Sourdough also improves your immune system against inflammation and gastrointestinal distress. Many people believe that the gluten present in sourdough can be bad for your gut health. However, as long as you don't have gluten intolerance, gluten can be beneficial for your gut and overall health.

Sourdough for a Healthier Lifestyle

Sourdough is beneficial for your health, whether it contains gluten or not.

It's Easier to Digest

The bacteria-yeast composition can help improve your gut and digestion process. The composition found in sourdough can break down the starch found in grains before it reaches your stomach, which means that your gut has less and easier work digesting it. Also, the fermentation process converts the enzymes in wheat, making the gluten more tolerant for many people.

Maintain Healthy Blood Sugar Range

Any carbohydrates naturally spike your glucose as they're being digested. While it's part of how the body works, some food and bread with high levels of sugar, especially when it lacks fibers or protein, can cause a sudden spike in blood glucose followed by a drop, increasing the risk of chronic illness. However, sourdough, because it's high in fiber and doesn't contain sugar, doesn't raise the glucose suddenly when digested.

Sourdough Options for Gluten-Free Diets

If you're gluten intolerant and your gut can't process traditional sourdough, you can make it gluten-free and enjoy all the benefits and easier baking process. Those who cannot tolerate gluten or are allergic to the protein from wheat, oats, and rye can switch to gluten-free sourdough without losing out on taste. It will still have the lactic acid bacteria found in traditional sourdough bread and pastries. These bacteria help produce compounds like antioxidants and anti-allergenic substances.

Gluten-Free Sourdough

You can easily create your gluten-free sourdough by creating a gluten-free starter and sourdough.

For the Starter:

Ingredients:

- Gluten-free flour blend
- Filtered water

Instructions:

1. Start whisking the gluten-free flour blend along with the filtered water. Keep whisking until the batter goes smooth.
2. Cover the bowl with a plate once you're done, but leave a small gap for the air to circulate.
3. Choose any two intervals during the day and add half a cup of water and flour in these intervals for 6 days. Make sure to whisk thoroughly at every interval until there are no bumps.
4. Once the mixture becomes bubbly and forms a dome on top of it, it is ready.

For the Sourdough:

Ingredients:

- **For the starter:** 2 cups of active sourdough starter
- **For the wet ingredients:** ⅔ cup of filtered water, 4 large, whisked eggs, ⅓ cup of oil

- **For the Dry Ingredients:** 1 ½ cups of sorghum flour, 1 cup of tapioca flour, 1 cup of oat milk, 1 cup of millet flour, 2 tablespoons of sugar, 1 tablespoon of salt.

Instructions:

1. Combine the starter and water in a bowl and start whisking. Slowly pour the eggs into the mix and continue whisking.
2. Whisk all the dry ingredients in another bowl.
3. Once the dry ingredients are mixed, slowly add the oil while continuing to stir.
4. If you're using a mixer, put it on low speed. If you're mixing by hand, try to be as smooth as possible while adding the wet ingredients to the dry mix. Keep mixing them slowly until they form a batter with no bumps. Make sure you always scrape the sides when mixing so you get an evenly mixed batter.
5. To allow the gluten-free flour to absorb the moisture, leave it in a warm area for 6 to 8 hours.
6. After letting it rest, divide the batter into three or four pieces based on your preferred loaf size.
7. If you're not planning to bake them all immediately, leave one outside and place the rest in the fridge.
8. Preheat your oven to 500°F (260°C) with a cast-iron Dutch oven inside for at least 30 minutes to ensure it's nice and hot.
9. Place the dough on a baking sheet, handling it gently to avoid deflation. Let it rest for another 4-8 hours.

Incorporating Whole Grains and Nutrients

Whole grains are a complete nutritional package compared to refined grains, which might lose nutrients during processing. Each whole-grain kernel has three parts: bran, germ, and endosperm, each offering health benefits.

- **Bran**: The outer layer is rich in fiber, Vitamin B, iron, copper, zinc, magnesium, antioxidants, and phytochemicals (natural plant compounds that may help prevent disease).
- **Germ**: The core of the seed. It's rich in healthy fats, vitamins E and B, and antioxidants.
- **Endosperm**: This inner layer provides carbohydrates, protein, and some B vitamins and minerals.

These components work together to benefit your health. Where fibers slow down the breakdown of starch into sugar, keeping your blood sugar steady and promoting digestive health by keeping you regular. On the other hand, phytochemicals and minerals can help lower cholesterol, prevent blood clots, and offer some protection against certain cancers.

Choosing whole grains over refined grains improves health in many ways. Here are some specific benefits:

- **Heart Health**: Whole grains can help lower bad cholesterol, triglycerides, and insulin levels, contributing to a healthier heart.
- **Diabetes Management**: This may help reduce the risk of type 2 diabetes by improving how your body uses insulin and regulates blood sugar.

- **Digestive Wellness**: The fiber in whole grains keeps you regular and may help prevent constipation and diverticular disease.

Including more whole grains in your diet and baking your sourdough with them is a simple yet powerful way to boost your overall health.

Whole Grain

20. The whole grain sourdough is packed with nutrients and beneficial resources. Source: https://www.pexels.com/photo/delicious-loaves-of-sourdough-bread-on-table-6605337/

Ingredients:

- 7 ounces water
- 7 ounces active sourdough starter
- 8.3 ounces whole wheat flour
- 9 ½ fluid ounces water
- 3 ounces rye flour

- 8.8 ounces white bread flour
- 6 ounces spelt flour
- 2.2 tsp salt

Instructions:

1. Combine the water, sourdough starter, and whole wheat flour in a large bowl. Mix well until a shaggy dough forms.
2. Cover the bowl loosely with plastic wrap and let it ferment at room temperature (around 69°F/20°C) for 12 hours.
3. Add the water, rye flour, white bread flour, spelt flour, and salt to the fermented dough.
4. Knead the dough until it becomes smooth and elastic. You can do this by hand for 10-15 minutes or with a stand mixer using the dough hook attachment for 5-7 minutes.
5. Place the kneaded dough in a clean bowl, cover it with plastic wrap, and refrigerate for 24 hours.
6. Remove the dough from the refrigerator and gently shape it into a round boule (loaf).
7. Place the boule on a lightly floured surface, seam side down, and cover it loosely with a clean cloth. Let it rise at room temperature (around 69°F/20°C) for 5 hours.
8. Preheat your oven to 485°F (250°C).
9. Once the dough has risen, gently transfer it to a baking sheet lined with parchment paper.

10. Bake for 40-45 minutes until the crust is golden brown and the internal temperature reaches around 205°F (96°C).
11. Let the bread cool completely on a wire rack before slicing and enjoying!

Making Sourdough Rich in Nutrients

If you're trying to lose or maintain your weight or want to increase your protein intake, adding protein to your sourdough can be a delicious and healthy way to eat your bread. This means that you're not just eating bread or sourdough pastries and benefiting from the dough but also increasing your protein intake during the day. Previous simple sourdough recipes contain between 2g and 12g per slice, depending on your ingredients and the size of your slice. However, adding more protein could take it to 20g to 25g.

Increasing your protein intake can:

- **Increase Satiety**: Protein can help you feel fuller for longer, potentially reducing cravings and aiding weight management.

- **Support an Active Lifestyle**: Athletes and those with physically demanding jobs may benefit from the extra protein for muscle building and recovery.

- **Dietary Preferences**: Some dietary restrictions might require a higher protein intake.

You can increase the protein in your sourdough by using high-protein flour, adding vital wheat gluten, seeds, and nuts, or using whey instead of water.

- **High-Protein Flours**: Experiment with flours like spelt, einkorn, or even commercially available high-protein bread flours.

- **High-Protein Starter**: You can also increase your protein intake by enhancing your starter and using high-protein flour such as whole wheat or rye instead of regular wheat.

- **Seeds and Grains**: For a protein and texture boost, include ingredients like sunflower seeds, chia seeds, or even cooked quinoa.

- **Cheese or Eggs**: While less common in sourdough, adding shredded cheese or a beaten egg during shaping can add protein and richness.

However, remember that when you're adding any source of protein, it will have an impact on texture and taste. Adding protein-rich ingredients can affect the final texture and flavor of your bread. Experiment with different amounts until you find what works best for your taste preferences. In addition, be mindful of fermentation time. Since protein can hinder gluten development, it's important not to over-ferment the dough. Keep in mind that shorter bulk fermentation times might be necessary.

More Tips and Tricks for High Fiber and Nutrient Sourdough

The sourdough bacteria need time to break down the wheat germ's outer shell for maximum nutritional benefit. To achieve this in a high-fiber bread, Many individuals found that a longer autolyze, followed by an hour of warm fermentation before a 36-hour cold-proof, results in a less dense and more moist loaf. The chia seeds contribute to this as well. This method also promotes a fantastic "ear" for those who appreciate the aesthetics of sourdough.

Warm Proofing for Cold Kitchens

If your kitchen runs cold, consider bulk fermenting and warming your dough in the oven with just the light on. This gentle heat provides enough warmth for the sourdough cultures to thrive, eliminating the need for a dedicated proofing oven. You'll be surprised by how much a whole-grain dough can rise with this method.

The Power of Fiber (7 grams per slice)

This high-fiber seeded sourdough gets its nutritional boost from a combination of whole wheat flour, spelt flour, and bulghur wheat. Here's a closer look at each ingredient:

Whole Wheat Flour

Working with whole wheat dough can be sticky throughout the process. Resist the urge to add extra flour during bulk fermentation. Instead, use wet hands for your stretch and folds until shaping.

Spelt Flour

An ancient whole grain, spelt flour is ground from the entire wheat head, including the bran layer. This bran is rich in B vitamins, fatty acids, protein, minerals, and fiber.

Bulghur Wheat

Bulghur wheat is a highly nutritious addition to your bread, a cracked whole-wheat grain commonly used in Mediterranean cuisine.

High-Fiber Seeded Sourdough

Ingredients:

- 12 ½ fluid ounces water (80 degrees Celsius)
- 3 ½ ounces levain
- 8.8 ounces bread flour
- 3 ½ ounces spelt flour
- 5.3 ounces whole wheat flour
- 1 ½ tsp salt
- 1 ½ ounces chia seeds
- 4 tsp sesame seeds
- 4 tsp bulgur wheat
- 5 ½ fluid ounces boiling water (for soaking seeds)

Instructions:

1. Whisk together the bread flour, spelt flour, whole wheat flour, and salt in a large bowl.
2. Add the lukewarm water and leaven to the dry ingredients. Mix well until a shaggy dough forms.
3. Cover the bowl loosely with plastic wrap or a damp cloth and let the dough rest at room temperature for 30 minutes.
4. After the autolyze, perform several sets of stretches and folds over 2-3 hours. You can do this every 30 minutes for a total of 4 sets.

5. While the dough develops, soak the chia seeds, sesame seeds, and bulgur wheat in boiling water for 30 minutes.
6. After the soaking period, drain the excess water from the seeds and mix them into the dough.
7. Cover the dough again and let it rise at room temperature for 6-8 hours or until doubled in size. During this time, bulk fermentation folds are done every few hours.
8. Gently shape the dough into a round boule on a lightly floured surface.
9. Place the shaped dough seam-side down in a floured banneton or bowl lined with a floured kitchen towel. Cover and let it rise at room temperature for 2-3 hours or until it has grown by about 50%.
10. At least 30 minutes before baking, preheat your oven to 500°F (260°C).
11. Before you start your baking process, gently score the top of the dough with a sharp knife.
12. Carefully transfer the dough to the preheated oven. Bake for 20 minutes with the lid on.
13. After 20 minutes, remove the lid and reduce the oven temperature to 450°F (230°C). Continue baking for another 20-25 minutes until the crust is golden brown and the internal temperature reaches around 205°F (96°C).
14. Let the bread cool completely on a wire rack before slicing and enjoying.

Ways to Increase Protein

Here are some easy ways to get great texture, flavor, and nutrition in sourdough bread, even when using a significant amount of high-protein white flour:

Hydration

High-protein flour needs more water than all-purpose flour. A good starting point is to increase the water ratio by 5-10% compared to the recipe's original flour weight. This added moisture helps create a softer and more tender loaf despite the increased gluten content. This mainly happens because of gluten development, which means more water creates a more flexible gluten network, resulting in a softer, airier crumb. It also impacts starch gelatinization. This means increased water allows the starches to gelatinize more thoroughly during baking, contributing to a softer texture.

Adding more water can make handling the dough trickier due to its stickier consistency. Start with a small increase and adjust as needed during future bakes.

Leverage the Autolyze Technique

The autolyze technique involves mixing flour and water and letting it rest. This simple step, especially with high-protein flour, allows enzymes, particularly protease, to break down protein bonds.

This breakdown makes the dough less elastic (prevents shrinking) and more extensible (stretches without tearing). This is crucial because high-protein flour can create a very elastic dough that's difficult to shape.

Minimize Mixing and Kneading

The dough needs less mixing and kneading due to the high gluten content than dough made with all-purpose flour. Shorter mixing times allow you to get the desired dough quicker.

Embrace Longer Fermentation

Dough with a higher protein content can tolerate longer fermentation without collapsing during baking. This is particularly true with sourdough starters or leavens. This allows for a longer final proof compared to dough made with lower-protein flour.

Chapter 7: Tips for Successful Sourdough Baking

Preparing sourdough is probably one of the hardest things in the culinary world. Many have tried, failed, and given up, but those who kept at it eventually succeeded. Trial and error is part of the baking process. This chapter will help you in your baking journey with effective time management tips, proper storage options, and the value of repurposing sourdough discards so that you will reach your destination sooner.

Time Management and Planning

As you may have noticed, timing is crucial in all sourdough recipes, whether the classic baking style or the artisanal variations. Sourdough relies on natural fermentation involving wild yeast and lactic acid bacteria. Proper fermentation is key to developing the dough's flavor, texture, and rise. Mismanaging time can result in over-fermented or under-fermented dough, making your bread too sour and dense or bland and flat.

As a beginner, you need consistency in baking to predict and control the outcomes. This is particularly necessary when refining your techniques and recipes. All your ingredients must be at their peak, especially the starter. This maximizes the leavening power and flavor development.

The baking process involves multiple steps interspersed with waiting periods while your dough ferments and proofs. If you do other tasks during this period, how will you know when the fermentation and proofing are done? How can you integrate these long waiting periods into your daily schedule and make the best use of your time?

Say you have to prepare the bread for a special event or family get-together. How can you plan your baking activities, so your contribution of bread is fresh?

If you are going to make a gift of sourdough bread, how can you ensure it is fresh out of the oven on gifting day? What if the dough and the ingredients go bad? How can you manage waste or prevent wastage altogether? The answers lie in time management and planning.

Understand the Baking Stages

Sourdough baking involves several stages: feeding the starter, mixing the dough, bulk fermentation, shaping, proofing, and baking. Each step requires specific timing.

- **Day 1 (Morning):** Feed your starter.

21. *The starter should look bright and creamy after being fed. Source: Anon423, CC BY-SA 4.0 <https://creativecommons.org/licenses/by-sa/4.0>, via Wikimedia Commons: https://commons.wikimedia.org/wiki/File:Carl_Griffith_sourdough_starter_stiff_just_fed_above.jpg*

- **Day 1 (Evening):** Mix the dough and let it rest (autolyze).

22. *Letting the dough rest is required after mixing the starter with water and flour. Source: William George James, CC BY-SA 4.0 <https://creativecommons.org/licenses/by-sa/4.0>, via Wikimedia Commons: https://commons.wikimedia.org/wiki/File:Mixing_Sourdough_starter_into_the_flour.jpg*

- **Day 1 (Night):** Knead and start bulk fermentation (with stretches and folds).
- **Day 2 (Morning):** Shape the dough and place it in the fridge for cold proofing.
- **Day 2 (Evening):** Bake the loaf.

Feed Your Starter Regularly

The microorganisms in the starter consume all available nutrients. Regular feedings keep the yeast and bacteria active and vigorous, giving it the required leavening power. It also prevents mold accumulation and contamination.

If you store it in the fridge, feed it once a week. Room temperature storage needs daily feeding. You should feed it twice in the days leading up to the bake. As a refresher, here are the feeding steps:

1. Remove a large portion of the starter
2. Add equal parts flour and water to feed it

Set Reminders

Set reminders on your phone or use a planner to keep track of each step. Forgetting even one of the steps, be it feeding, kneading, fermenting, or proofing, can result in substandard bread.

Prepare in Advance

Prepare a list of all the ingredients and utensils ready beforehand. You will need bread flour, any other specialty flour, water, salt, mixing bowls, proofing baskets, an active starter, and your baking setup.

Utilize Downtime

During the waiting period of bulk fermentation and proofing, you can clean up, prepare other meals, or complete other tasks. Set regular reminders to check if the fermentation is going well or if proofing is progressing steadily.

Plan around Your Day

It's even better to integrate the sourdough process into your daily routine. Reserve the long waiting processes for when you're working or sleeping. For example, you can start the bulk fermentation before bed and let it ferment overnight. Cold-proof the dough before heading to work the next day so you will find it ready when you return home.

Alternatively, if you prefer to be awake during fermentation, you can speed it up by keeping it at room temperature. Proofing time can also be reduced this way. This flexibility in the waiting period is especially useful during emergencies when you can prevent your partly-made sourdough from going to waste.

Record Your Process

Keep a baking journal to note down what works and what doesn't. Make sure you record times, temperatures, and any changes you make. This helps you refine your process over time.

Batch Baking

If possible, bake more than one loaf at the same time. This saves time and energy, as the preparation steps are the same for one loaf or several.

Sample Sourdough Baking Schedule

Day before Baking:

- **8 AM:** Feed the starter
- **6 PM:** Mix the dough (autolyze)
- **7 PM:** Add salt and start bulk fermentation (stretch and fold every 30 minutes for two hours)
- **9 PM:** Let the dough ferment overnight

Baking Day:

- **7 AM:** Shape the dough and place it in the proofing basket
- **8 AM:** Put the dough in the fridge for cold-proofing
- **5 PM:** Preheat the oven and bake the bread

Proper Storage of Sourdough

As you might know, a sourdough loaf lasts longer than most other types of bread because of its natural acidity. However, it will become stale after five days, so if you plan to eat it a week after baking (or more), you will need to store it properly. Its crisp crust is most appetizing and more prone to going stale. The crumb inside, usually soft and chewy, will dry out as time passes. Mold will grow on the bread if you store it in humid or airtight containers.

Sourdough bread has a special flavor due to the natural fermentation process. However, its characteristic taste and smell may decline even before the bread becomes stale. Improper storage can speed up the process even more. For example, if you store it in a plastic bag at room temperature, it may start giving off an unpleasant smell in a couple of days.

Economically, preserving the loaf instead of eating it right away makes sense. You have spent a lot of time and money in preparation and high-quality ingredients. Proper storage ensures you get the most out of your investment by extending the bread's usability.

Furthermore, it will be easier and more convenient to plan your meals if you have sourdough bread stored away. What if your cousins who love sourdough pastries suddenly decide to visit you? Your child may crave a pizza in the middle of the night when no store is open. You may run out of breakfast options one fine morning. Rest assured, you will have many uses for your stored sourdough bread, and proper storage helps it stay fresh and retain its texture and flavor.

Short-Term Storage (One to Two Days)

This storage technique keeps the bread for five days. However, the bread will not be at its best after about two to three days and might be turning.

Wrap the fresh sourdough bread in a clean kitchen towel or place it in a breathable bread bag. This helps keep the crust crisp while preventing the bread from drying out too quickly. Avoid storing it in plastic bags as they trap moisture, making the crust soggy and the bread more prone to mold. Another option is to store it in a paper bag, which allows some airflow to maintain the crust while protecting the bread from becoming too dry.

Medium-Term Storage (Up to One Week)

Are you planning a small party or a big gathering within a week? A bread box provides a balanced environment, with the tiny slits giving some airflow while protecting the bread from excessive dryness and maintaining a good crust texture. Store the bread cut-side down on a cutting board or inside the bread box. This helps to reduce moisture loss from the exposed crumb.

Long-Term Storage (More than 1 Week)

If you don't plan to eat the sourdough bread soon, the best and only option is to freeze it. However, don't place the whole loaf in the freezer. What if you want to munch on small bites or use part of the loaf for making pastries? Cut it into slices so you don't need to thaw the entire loaf every time.

Wrap the bread tightly in aluminum foil, then place it in a heavy-duty freezer bag or an airtight container to protect it from freezer burn. Don't forget to label and date the packages to keep track of storage times since the bread will last no longer than six months.

Thawing and Refreshing

When you freeze sourdough bread, it's as if you're slowing down time. It will retain its nutrients, flavors, and freshness until removed from the freezer. However, you won't experience the flavors and freshness if you eat it right out of the freezer.

Let it thaw (keeping it covered) at room temperature for a few hours. If you're planning to have it the next day, remove the slices from the freezer before hitting the hay and let them thaw overnight. Place the slices directly into a toaster if you want them even quicker.

Preheat your oven to 350°F (176°C) to refresh the crust. Lightly mist the bread with water and place it directly on the oven rack for about 10 minutes. Whole loaves should be wrapped in foil and heated in the oven for 20 minutes. Remove the foil for the last five minutes to crisp up the crust.

Quick Tips

- Avoid refrigerating the sourdough bread. It can go stale faster due to the starch retrogradation process (water is retained, but freshness is lost). It's better to store at room temperature or freeze for longer storage.

- Keep the bread in a cool, dry place, away from direct sunlight and heat sources, to prevent it from drying out or molding.

- Regularly check your stored bread for signs of mold. Discard the bread immediately to avoid contamination if any mold appears (black to white spots or stains).

Reviving and Repurposing Sourdough Discards

While feeding your sourdough starter, you discard a large portion of it. You can revive and repurpose it instead of throwing it away or composting it. By repurposing, you reduce food waste.

Using discards maximizes the use of the ingredients you've invested in. Did you know that the particular tang of sourdough bread comes from the starter? The discarded part of the starter also retains the flavor, which you can use in other recipes. It can also be used as a main ingredient in other dishes instead of just a flavoring agent.

The discard can improve the texture and moisture content of baked goods. Sourdough fermentation can increase the bioavailability of nutrients in flour, making the resulting products potentially more nutritious. If you repurpose the discard regularly, you won't need to set reminders to feed the starter. It will stay at a manageable size, and you won't be wasting the discard.

Once you know how to repurpose the discard, try to experiment with new dishes that will improve your culinary skills. Other recipes using sourdough discard benefit from its natural leavening and flavor properties. The recipes are often quicker and easier than making traditional sourdough loaves.

Reviving and repurposing sourdough discards is a great way to minimize waste and create delicious, versatile baked goods. The process of reviving is the same as feeding the starter. Mix the discard with equal parts of flour and water (by weight) to feed the natural yeast and bacteria. Then, let it sit at room temperature for several hours until it becomes bubbly and active again. You can also let it sit overnight.

Repurposing

Once you have revived the sourdough discard, you can repurpose it in many recipes you learned in Chapter 4. It will give those dishes the distinct tang of sourdough. Here's a short refresher:

- **Sourdough Pancakes:** Mix discard with flour, milk, eggs, baking soda, and a touch of sugar to make fluffy, tangy pancakes.

- **Sourdough Waffles:** Similar to pancakes, add discard to your waffle batter for extra depth of flavor.

- **Sourdough Crackers:** Combine discard with flour, olive oil, salt, and herbs or spices of your choice. Roll the dough thinly and bake until crispy.

- **Banana Bread:** Incorporate sourdough discard into banana bread batter for a unique twist.

- **Muffins:** Add discard to muffin recipes for extra moisture and flavor.

- **Flatbreads:** Mix discard with flour, water, and salt to create a simple dough for making flatbreads.

- **Pizza Dough:** Use discard to enhance the flavor of your pizza dough.

- **Biscuits:** Discard can be added to the biscuit dough for a tangy flavor.

- **Scones:** Add discard to scone recipes for a moist and flavorful treat.

- **Sourdough Brownies:** Use discard in your brownie batter for a rich, complex flavor.

- **Cookies:** Mix discard into cookie dough for a tangy twist on traditional recipes.

- **Fritters:** Add discard to vegetable or seafood fritter batter for extra tang.

- **Tempura:** Use discard to make a light and crispy tempura batter.

Example Recipes

Sourdough Crackers

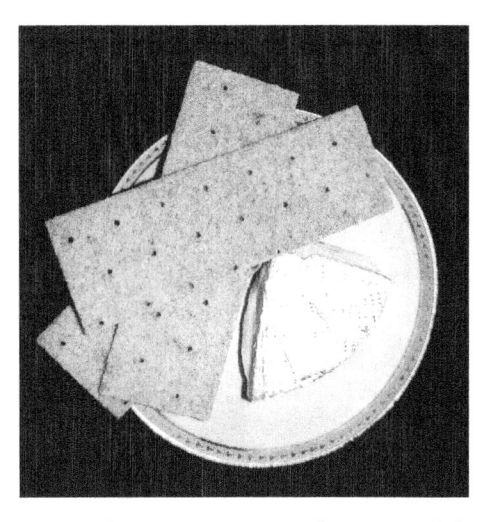

23. What better to make your tasty crackers out of than sourdough? Source: Daderot, CC0, via Wikimedia Commons: https://commons.wikimedia.org/wiki/File:Camembert_and_sourdough_rye_crisps_-_Massachusetts.jpg

Add the unique sourdough tang to your regular salty crackers.

Ingredients:

- 1 cup sourdough discard
- 1 cup flour
- 1/4 cup olive oil
- 1/2 teaspoon salt
- Herbs, spices, seeds for topping (optional)

Instructions:

1. Preheat the oven to 350°F (176°C).

2. Mix all ingredients in a bowl until a dough forms.
3. Roll out the dough thinly on a floured surface.
4. Cut into desired shapes and place on a baking sheet.
5. Bake for 15-20 minutes or until golden and crisp.

Sourdough Scones

24. A sourdough scone is a quick, healthy option if you are on the go. Source: https://pixabay.com/photos/scone-flour-salt-sos-cheese-3871598/

Transform your sweet and crumbly scone into a sour and tangy confectionary.

Ingredients:

- 2 cups all-purpose flour
- 1/4 cup granulated sugar
- 1 tablespoon baking powder
- 1/2 teaspoon salt
- 1/2 cup unsalted butter, cold and cut into cubes
- 1 cup sourdough discard (unfed)

- 1/4 cup (60ml) heavy cream or milk
- 1 large egg
- 1 teaspoon vanilla extract

Instructions:

1. Preheat your oven to 400°F (204°C), and line a baking sheet with a baking mat.
2. Whisk the flour, sugar, baking powder, and salt in a bowl.
3. Add the cold, cubed butter to the flour mixture.
4. Mix the sourdough discard, heavy cream (or milk), egg, and vanilla extract in a separate bowl. Note that the discard isn't revived, only repurposed.
5. Pour the wet ingredients into the dry ingredients. Stir gently until the dough is slightly sticky and shaggy.
6. Turn the dough out onto a lightly floured surface. Gently pat it into a round, inch-thick disk.
7. Cut the disk into eight wedges using a knife or bench scraper.
8. Transfer the wedges to the prepared baking sheet, spacing them apart to allow for spreading.
9. Bake in the preheated oven for 15-20 minutes or until the scones are golden brown and a toothpick inserted into the center comes out clean.
10. Allow the scones to cool on the baking sheet for a few minutes before transferring them to a wire rack to cool completely.

Chapter 8: Sourdough for All: Inclusive and Accessible

Baking any bread may seem difficult for a novice, much less sourdough bread. No wonder most people prefer to buy loaves from the baker. However, this cookbook's easy instructions and simple visuals would have begun to change your mind. Granted, baking takes time, but once you get into the flow of things, you can easily incorporate the process into your daily schedule.

How Sourdough Is Inclusive and Accessible for All

Consider the basic ingredients for sourdough - flour, water, and salt. They are inexpensive and widely available. Head to the smallest market in your vicinity, and you will find flour and salt at a reasonable price. Turn on the tap or buy bottled water; regardless of your economic status, you can bake sourdough loaves with little practice.

Specialized equipment can be beneficial. You will find many uses for kitchen scales, oven mitts, stand mixers, fermentation weights, dough whisks, thermometers, a Dutch oven, and more. However, you don't particularly need these things. You can easily make do with basic kitchen tools like a stirring utensil, a cooling rack, parchment paper, a regular oven, and clean containers.

Diet-conscious people often look down on bread, but sourdough bread can be made gluten-free with whole wheat flour and is just as tangy and chewy. You don't need to compromise on your diet to incorporate it into your daily breakfast.

No part of the recipe ever goes to waste. Even the starter discards can be revived and repurposed to make more bread or many delicious desserts and pastries. If you don't want to make any more, give them to your friends and family who are baking enthusiasts and see their eyes light up.

Sourdough baking is a skill anyone can learn, regardless of their background. If you are ever stuck or can't get past a certain process, a quick look at the recipe or troubleshooting section in this book will help you progress. Additionally, many online forums, social media groups, and websites are dedicated to sourdough baking where people worldwide share tips, recipes, and support. Many communities offer free or low-cost sourdough baking classes and workshops as well.

Sourdough baking isn't about technique. It's an art that allows for a high degree of personalization. You can experiment with different flours, hydration levels, and processes to create a product that reflects your preferences. Let your imagination soar with personalized scoring patterns that showcase your creativity.

Your exploration journey continues through different cultural bread-making traditions that help you understand and appreciate diverse culinary practices. The bread is easier to digest than commercially yeasted bread, which helps if you have digestive issues. You can control the ingredients, avoid additives and preservatives in store-bought bread, and make your variant as healthy and tangy as possible.

Sourdough baking inadvertently benefits the social and natural environment. It encourages using locally sourced flours and ingredients, supports local farmers, and reduces the carbon footprint associated with transportation. It often involves using up all parts of the grain and can incorporate food scraps (like vegetable peels) into the dough, promoting a zero-waste approach.

While mastering sourdough can take time, beginners can achieve good results with basic techniques detailed in Chapters 2 and 3, and more advanced bakers can continually challenge themselves with more complex methods mentioned in the later chapters.

While sourdough baking is definitely inclusive for all, what about this cookbook? Can you recommend it to someone who has never even boiled an egg? Can baking enthusiasts find it insightful?

User-Friendly Design for All Skill Levels

Are you a beginner, a mid-level baker, or an expert cook who only wants to learn about sourdough bread? If you found this cookbook helpful, other people with similar skill levels will also enjoy it. It has a user-friendly design that is structured to be appealing to any creative eye.

The chapter titles and subsections are created to find exactly what you're looking for without having to read every page. Simply check the index if you want to find the classic sourdough recipe or a health-conscious option. It doesn't matter if you are a beginner or an expert; you can find and learn everything about sourdough in this user-friendly book.

You will have noticed the structure has been organized logically. The book starts with a brief introduction, an overview of the sourdough world, the basic requirements, the classic and advanced recipes, other products you can make, the different flavors and health-conscious options, and a number of helpful tips. As a beginner, you won't get confused with the flow of the book, and intermediate cooks can browse through the index to find what they are looking for.

The recipes are flexible enough to suit all your requirements. There is a plain sourdough recipe, its advanced variations, add-ons you can try out, different shapes of loaves and scoring patterns, and numerous flavors that can satisfy all kinds of taste buds. It's not like the advanced variations can only be used by intermediate to expert-level cooks. The easy instructions with vivid imagery ensure that people of all skill levels can enjoy baking.

The best part is that you can experiment with your own recipes. Once you get the hang of all the recipes mentioned in this book, you can try adding other ingredients that will enhance the taste and useability of your sourdough. The content is engaging enough to inspire even the least motivated individual to start baking their first sourdough loaf. It emphasizes the importance of failure and to keep trying until you can bake the fluffy and chewy bread with the tangy taste you long for.

Are you facing problems despite following all the instructions? Does your bread lack the required tang? Are there large gaps in its structure? Isn't it rising enough, resulting in a flat, stale-looking loaf? The troubleshooting section in Chapter 3 has got you covered.

It explores every little problem you may face while baking and explains feasible solutions to tackle it. From increasing the proofing time to strengthening the starter, it helps you navigate the complex waters of the recipes to bake your first perfect sourdough bread. Check out Chapter 7, which also provides tips on managing your baking time so you can do other tasks without compromising on the sourdough process.

Ultimately, the book is designed so anyone can read and understand it regardless of skill level. The images are bright, the instructions are concise, and the overall design is user-friendly. A lot of thought and effort has been put into coming up with this design that appeals to everyone. Even the little things, like the fonts, have been carefully chosen, which brings you to the next section.

Large Fonts and Clear Instructions

Most cookbooks focus only on the actual recipe. However, it doesn't matter how good the recipe is if you find it hard to read. That is where the fonts and the clarity of instructions come into the picture. As you may have noticed, the recipes in this cookbook are functional, useful, easily doable, and pristine. That's partly because of the large fonts used.

Large fonts reduce eye strain and make reading the text easier for readers of all ages and visual abilities. Bakers can quickly glance at the instructions while working, allowing them to keep their focus on the dough without losing their place in the recipe. Indeed, this book is accessible to people with visual impairments or reading difficulties, too, ensuring that more people can enjoy and use it effectively.

You can adjust the font size better in the eBook because of the already large font. No matter how much you increase the size, there won't be any visible pixels, making it ideal for people who need even larger text. The layout is clean and professional, which makes the book easier to navigate.

Clear, step-by-step instructions break down the baking process into manageable sub-recipes, which is especially helpful for beginners. It helps you reduce misunderstandings and mistakes, leading to more successful baking experiences. With these easy-to-follow steps, you will feel more confident in your abilities, so you won't hesitate to try any new recipes that you come up with.

The recipes mentioned in this book will consistently give you the same result once you are successful, thanks to the step-by-step guide with a large font. It will be difficult to miss a single step, no matter how hard you try! You can follow them more efficiently, saving time and effort during baking. They will eliminate the guesswork, too, making the process smoother and more enjoyable.

A cookbook with large fonts and clear instructions is more manageable. It will motivate you to try all the recipes mentioned and again if you fail. Many cookbooks have a tiny font to accommodate the images and the extensive list of instructions. This book doesn't compromise on the quality of the knowledge contained or how it is presented. The positive experiences with clear, readable instructions will encourage you to keep using the cookbook and recommend it to others.

Imagine you don't care about cooking but just want to try your hand at improving your skills. If you start reading a book with a tiny font and haphazard instructions, you may not even go beyond the introduction, no matter how interesting the content is. Clear instructions and readable text help bakers of all levels understand the processes and techniques involved, aiding in skill development and improvement while keeping them hooked throughout.

Mistakes are a part of every baking process. Even expert cooks are prone to mistakes. However, with straightforward instructions, you will be able to identify your mistakes easily and correct them. You will learn and evolve your technique quicker to bake a delicious sourdough loaf for you and your family in no time.

Giving this book as a gift? Whoever receives it their experience with the book will be significantly enhanced. The quality and accessibility of the content make this cookbook the best gift you ever give them! Think about it: you read it until this point, regardless of your background. Would you have kept on reading if the font had been small and the instructions were barely readable?

Vibrant Images for Visual Guidance

Imagine reading a sourdough cookbook that is entirely textual with no images. The instructions are clear, the font is large, and the design is user-friendly. However, you have never seen a sourdough bread and don't know about any kitchen utensils or ingredients.

So, when you are instructed to prepare the starter, which can be described as "a living wild yeast," your imagination will go haywire. Is wild yeast a living, breathing creature you need to maintain as a pet? Is it alive enough to hurt you? How can you catch it, and where will you keep it?

Without a proper image showing a harmless sourdough starter (which looks nothing like a living creature), people may be scared off from following the recipe. Words can be easily misinterpreted, but images tell a factual story that cannot be misconstrued.

The vibrant images included in this cookbook play a major role in guiding you visually on your journey, enhancing your overall experience and skill.

- **Step-by-Step Visuals:** Images illustrating each step of the process help clarify written instructions, making them easier to understand and follow along.

- **Techniques Demonstration:** Visuals can demonstrate specific techniques, such as kneading, shaping, and scoring, which are often better understood through images than text alone.

- **End Product Visualization:** Photos of the final product show you how the result should be, setting clear expectations for the appearance and texture of your bread. For instance, you don't want your bread to be too fluffy or too flat, but without a frame of reference to compare against, you may not realize the right structure and rise.

- **Intermediate Stages:** Images of the dough at various stages (e.g., mixing, proofing, baking) help you recognize whether you are on the right track. Are you kneading the dough properly? How should it look after you have stretched and folded it a few times? What exactly happens after proofing?

- **Visual Learning Aid:** Many people learn better through visual aids. Images can enhance comprehension and retention of the steps and techniques involved in sourdough baking.

- **Mistake Identification:** By comparing your dough or bread to the images, you can identify mistakes and make necessary adjustments. For instance, you may need an image to understand how big the holes or gaps in your loaf should be.

- **Aesthetic Appeal:** Vibrant, high-quality images make this cookbook more visually appealing. The instructions were clear, and the content was interesting, but the images were part of the reason you kept reading.

- **Inspiration:** Beautiful photos of the final products can inspire you to experiment with different recipes and techniques, boosting your creativity for an even better picture of bread.

- **Visual Confirmation:** Seeing each step visually confirmed in images can boost your confidence, reassuring you that you are following the process correctly.

- **Error Reduction:** Visual cues help minimize errors by providing a clear reference point, reducing the chances of misinterpreting written instructions.

- **Ingredient Identification:** With the images of ingredients and tools, you can correctly identify what you need and avoid mistakes. For example, if you use the wrong kind of flour, the taste of the bread may not be what you expect.

- **Process Understanding:** Photos of the dough's progression through different stages provide context. You can understand how the dough should change over time.

Indeed, novice bakers will benefit greatly from images in this book that will show them exactly what to do and what to look for. Even experienced bakers can refine their skills and techniques by closely examining the detailed images of more advanced processes. Vibrant images add a sensory dimension to the cookbook, making baking more enjoyable and engaging.

You can quickly browse through the cookbook and select recipes that appeal to you. You can also compare different recipes, helping you choose based on difficulty.

Unless you are a cook or simply have a passion for baking, you were most likely inspired to purchase this book from the pictures and videos of lip-smacking sourdough loaves you saw in your social media feed.

Conclusion

Sourdough bread only seems difficult to bake, but with the help of the recipes you learned so far, the process will be a breeze. To simplify the process even further, here's a brief summary of everything you learned in this book.

You started by diving into the world of sourdough with an informative overview and the dish's unique features, like its tangy taste and chewy texture. You learned the most important ingredient of the bread - the sourdough starter. It is a mixture of yeast and bacteria that takes around 10 days to prepare. So, if you want to make sourdough bread for a party, you will need to prepare the starter well in advance.

The main classic recipe requires an oven, preferably the Dutch version with steam, along with a few other ingredients and equipment. It doesn't matter if you have never baked anything in your life, but having some experience helps. If you fail, you can always try again, and you won't even need to go through the 10-day starter preparation because you can revive and reuse the discards.

The classic sourdough recipe isn't difficult at all, thanks to the two processes that give you some respite from the rigorous baking - bulk fermentation and proofing. Many of the baking issues can be easily resolved, and a few others can enhance the process instead of harming it. Additionally, you can make a number of other delicacies with the starter and bread, like pancakes, waffles, pastries, pizza crusts, and more!

Are you tired of the regular tang of the bread? Switch it up with herbs and spices or cheese-infused products. You can also add fruits and nuts or come up with unique flavor combinations of your own. You later learned how to live a healthy lifestyle with gluten-free sourdough and recipes including whole grains and nutrients.

Near the end, several tips for incorporating sourdough baking into your daily routine were discussed, along with some excellent storing techniques and the processes of reviving discards. Indeed, sourdough is inclusive and accessible for everyone, not just while eating but for baking too. People of all ages and skill levels can indulge in this art.

Key Takeaways

- The basic ingredients for the classic recipe are sourdough starter, water, bread flour, and salt.
- You can add more ingredients like seeds and nuts.
- You can mix different types of flours like rye, whole wheat, spelt, and einkorn.
- Revive and repurpose the discarded sourdough starter whenever you can for more bread, desserts, and other delights.

References

10 Sourdough Myths Debunked. (n.d.). You Knead Sourdough. https://www.youkneadsourdough.com.au/blogs/sourdough-stories/10-sourdough-myths-debunked

Amy. (2024, June 10). Easy sourdough flatbread recipe with active starter or discard – no yeast. A Blossoming Life. https://ablossominglife.com/easy-sourdough-flatbread-recipe/

Amy. (2024, May 4). Three Cheese Sourdough Bread. Amy Bakes Bread. https://amybakesbread.com/three-cheese-sourdough-bread/

Awais, M. (2022, October 14). Whole Food Earth® | Whole Food Earth®. Wholefoodearth.com. https://wholefoodearth.com/wholesome/benefits-of-making-bread-at-home.

Bass, L. (2023, October 17). How to Store Sourdough Bread To Keep It Fresh. Farmhouse on Boone. https://www.farmhouseonboone.com/how-to-store-sourdough-bread/

Bass, L. (2024, March 6). Beginner's sourdough bread recipe. Farmhouse on Boone. https://www.farmhouseonboone.com/beginners-sourdough-bread-recipe/

Bass, L. (2024a, March 6). Easy sourdough puff pastry. Farmhouse on Boone. https://www.farmhouseonboone.com/easy-sourdough-puff-pastry/

Bass, L. (2024b, March 6). Sourdough pastry braid. Farmhouse on Boone. https://www.farmhouseonboone.com/sourdough-pastry-braid/

Bettie, B. (2021, June 28). Understanding sourdough starter: Feeding, ratios, using in dough, leaven. Baker Bettie.

https://bakerbettie.com/understanding-sourdough-starter-feeding-ratios-using-in-dough-leaven/

Blythman, J., & Sykes, R. (2013, June 22). Why sourdough bread is good for you. The Guardian.
https://www.theguardian.com/lifeandstyle/2013/jun/22/sourdough-bread-good-for-you

Countryroadssourdough. (2023, March 24). 21 Sourdough Flavor Ideas. Country Roads Sourdough.
https://countryroadssourdough.com/21sourdoughaddins/

Currier, H. (2022, November 27). Sourdough bread basics: A beginner's guide. Mom Loves Baking. https://www.momlovesbaking.com/sourdough-bread-basics-a-beginners-guide/

Duska, A. (2023, February 10). Sourdough waffles (or pancakes). Little Spoon Farm. https://littlespoonfarm.com/sourdough-pancakes-waffles-recipe/

Duska, A. (2024, March 22). Sourdough pizza crust. Little Spoon Farm. https://littlespoonfarm.com/sourdough-pizza-crust-recipe/

Dwyer, M. (2023, September 4). The Benefits of Gluten-Free Sourdough to Our Microbiome and Digestive Health. Bread SRSLY.
https://breadsrsly.com/blogs/blog/sourdough-microbiome-benefits

Eby, M. (2022, September 29). This Sourdough Whisperer Will Help You Solve Your Bread Problems. Food & Wine.
https://www.foodandwine.com/cooking-techniques/baking/this-sourdough-whisperer-nora-allen-mel-bakery

Estrada, J. (2022, November 29). Everything you need to know about Sourdough starter. Bread & Basil.
https://www.breadandbasil.nyc/sourdough/sourdough-starter#levain=

Exploring Flavor Variations in Sourdough – What is Olivia Learning? (n.d.). Olivianewman.opened.ca.
https://olivianewman.opened.ca/2023/12/10/exploring-flavor-variations-in-sourdough/

foodbodsourdough, A. (2023, April 25). Gummy loaves. The Simplest Way to Make Sourdough. https://foodbodsourdough.com/gummy-loaves/

Hamel, P. (n.d.). Classic sourdough pancakes or waffles. King Arthur Baking. https://www.kingarthurbaking.com/recipes/classic-sourdough-waffles-or-pancakes-recipe

Jennings, K.-A. (2016). 9 Legitimate Health Benefits of Eating Whole Grains. Healthline. https://www.healthline.com/nutrition/9-benefits-of-whole-grains

Leo, M. (2020, March 16). The Best Way to Store Bread | The Perfect Loaf. Www.theperfectloaf.com. https://www.theperfectloaf.com/the-best-way-to-store-bread/

Leo, M. (2023, January 13). High-fiber seeded sourdough bread recipe | The Perfect Loaf. Www.theperfectloaf.com. https://www.theperfectloaf.com/high-fiber-sourdough-bread-recipe/

Leo, M. (2024a, May 2). Beginner's sourdough bread. The Perfect Loaf. https://www.theperfectloaf.com/beginners-sourdough-bread/

Leo, M. (2024b, May 16). The Ultimate Sourdough Starter Guide. The Perfect Loaf. https://www.theperfectloaf.com/guides/sourdough-starter/

luxfordnutri. (2022, November 7). Benefits of Sourdough Bread (Plus my gluten-free starter recipe!). Luxford Nutrition. https://luxfordnutrition.com/benefits-of-sourdough-bread

Mama, T. P. (2020a, June 6). Coffee Sourdough Bread with Maple Infused Dates. The Pantry Mama. https://www.pantrymama.com/sourdough-bread-with-coffee-maple-infused-dates/

Mama, T. P. (2020a, November 14). How to Get A Thinner Crust on Sourdough Bread And Make It Softer & Less Chewy. The Pantry Mama. https://www.pantrymama.com/thinner-crust-sourdough/

Mama, T. P. (2020b, December 1). Sourdough Hydration for Beginners: Easy Explanation. The Pantry Mama. https://www.pantrymama.com/understanding-hydration-in-sourdough-bread-baking/

Mama, T. P. (2020b, July 12). Flavored Sourdough: How To Make Additions To Sourdough Bread. The Pantry Mama. https://www.pantrymama.com/flavored-sourdough/

Mama, T. P. (2021, November 23). Adding Sugar to Sourdough Bread: Is It Necessary? The Pantry Mama. https://www.pantrymama.com/adding-sugar-to-sourdough-bread/

Mariah. (2024, May 10). Sourdough Danish pastries: A recipe from the farm. TheFarmChicken. https://thefarmchicken.com/sourdough-danish-pastries-a-recipe-from-the-farm/

McKenna. (2023, May 5). Sourdough flatbread recipe (with active starter or discard). Simplicity and a Starter. https://simplicityandastarter.com/sourdough-flatbread-recipe/#Ingredients

Mel. (2024, March 28). Easy sourdough flatbread. Mel's Kitchen Cafe. https://www.melskitchencafe.com/easy-sourdough-flatbread/

Nowland, L. (2020, June 18). Sourdough - Why it's so wonderful -. Nurture from Within. https://nurturefromwithin.com.au/sourdough-why-its-so-wonderful

Pichler, P. (2021, September 22). The dough also rises: the joy of baking bread. Taffeta. https://taffeta.com/the-dough-also-rises-the-joy-of-baking-bread

Raffa, E. (2014, January 3). Sourdough Bread: A Beginner's Guide. The Clever Carrot. https://www.theclevercarrot.com/2014/01/sourdough-bread-a-beginners-guide/#sourdough-recipe

Raffa, E. (2014, January 3). Sourdough Bread: A Beginner's Guide. The Clever Carrot. https://www.theclevercarrot.com/2014/01/sourdough-bread-a-beginners-guide/

Raffa, E. (2014, January 3). Sourdough Bread: A Beginner's Guide. The Clever Carrot. https://www.theclevercarrot.com/2014/01/sourdough-bread-a-beginners-guide/

Raffa, E. (2020, June 7). Light Whole Wheat Sourdough Bread. The Clever Carrot. https://www.theclevercarrot.com/2020/06/whole-wheat-sourdough-bread/

Raffa, E. (2020, October 18). Sourdough Discard 101: Recipes & FAQs Answered. The Clever Carrot. https://www.theclevercarrot.com/2020/10/sourdough-discard-101-recipes-faqs-answered-pancakes/

Sam. (2024, January 23). Sourdough pizza crust. Sugar Spun Run. https://sugarspunrun.com/sourdough-pizza-crust/

Sourdough bread scoring tutorial - how to score like a pro | Foodgeek. (2019, July 27). Foodgeek.dk. https://foodgeek.dk/en/sourdough-bread-scoring-tutorial/

Sourdough Discard Recipes | King Arthur Baking. (n.d.). Www.kingarthurbaking.com. https://www.kingarthurbaking.com/recipes/collections/sourdough-discard-recipes

Swathi. (2019, August 27). Turmeric Sourdough Bread. Zesty South Indian Kitchen. https://zestysouthindiankitchen.com/turmeric-sourdough-bread/

Swathi. (2023, December 3). 52 Sourdough bread with various Add-ins. Zesty South Indian Kitchen. https://zestysouthindiankitchen.com/52-sourdough-bread-with-various-add-ins/

The Ultimate Guide to Gluten Free Sourdough | Best in Gluten Free. (n.d.). Schär. https://www.schaer.com/en-us/a/gluten-free-sourdough-guide

Trend or Truth: Is Sourdough Bread Actually Healthier? (n.d.). Wellness with Kaelyn. https://wellnesswithkaelyn.com/blog/sourdough-bread-actually-healthier

Whole Grains. (2014, January 24). The Nutrition Source. https://nutritionsource.hsph.harvard.edu/what-should-you-eat/whole-grains/

WHY CHOOSE GLUTEN FREE SOURDOUGH. (2022, March 4). The Gluten Free Bakery. https://www.mygfbakery.com/blogs/gluten-free-living/why-choose-gluten-free-sourdough

Printed in Great Britain
by Amazon